EASY TO BUILD BIRDHOUSES
a natural approach

A.J. HAMLER

POPULAR WOODWORKING BOOKS
CINCINNATI, OHIO
www.popularwoodworking.com

READ THIS IMPORTANT SAFETY NOTICE

To prevent accidents, keep safety in mind while you work. Use the safety guards installed on power equipment; they are for your protection.

When working on power equipment, keep fingers away from saw blades, wear safety goggles to prevent injuries from flying wood chips and sawdust, wear hearing protection and consider installing a dust vacuum to reduce the amount of airborne sawdust in your woodshop.

Don't wear loose clothing, such as neckties or shirts with loose sleeves, or jewelry, such as rings, necklaces or bracelets, when working on power equipment. Tie back long hair to prevent it from getting caught in your equipment.

People who are sensitive to certain chemicals should check the chemical content of any product before using it.

Due to the variability of local conditions, construction materials, skill levels, etc., neither the author nor Popular Woodworking Books assumes any responsibility for any accidents, injuries, damages or other losses incurred resulting from the material presented in this book.

The authors and editors who compiled this book have tried to make the contents as accurate and correct as possible. Plans, illustrations, photographs and text have been carefully checked. All instructions, plans and projects should be carefully read, studied and understood before beginning construction.

Prices listed for supplies and equipment were current at the time of publication and are subject to change.

METRIC CONVERSION CHART

to convert	to	multiply by
Inches	Centimeters	2.54
Centimeters	Inches	0.4
Feet	Centimeters	30.5
Centimeters	Feet	0.03
Yards	Meters	0.9
Meters	Yards	1.1

Distributed in Canada by Fraser Direct
100 Armstrong Avenue
Georgetown, Ontario L7G 5S4
Canada

Distributed in the U.K. and Europe by David & Charles
Brunel House
Newton Abbot
Devon TQ12 4PU
England
Tel: (+44) 1626 323200
Fax: (+44) 1626 323319
E-mail: postmaster@davidandcharles.co.uk

Distributed in Australia by Capricorn Link
P.O. Box 704
Windsor, NSW 2756
Australia

Visit our Web site at www.popularwoodworking.com.

Other fine Popular Woodworking Books are available from your local bookstore or direct from the publisher.

14   13   12   11   5   4

Library of Congress Cataloging-in-Publication Data

Hamler, A. J. (Anthony J.), 1951-
   Easy to build birdhouses : a natural approach / A.J. Hamler. -- 1st ed.
      p. cm.
   ISBN 978-1-4403-0220-6 (pbk. : alk. paper)
   1. Birdhouses--Design and construction. I. Title.
   QL676.5.H326 2010
   690'.8927--dc22

                                              2010001391

ACQUISITIONS EDITOR: David Thiel
SENIOR EDITOR: Jim Stack
DESIGNER: Brian Roeth
PRODUCTION COORDINATOR: Mark Griffin
PHOTOGRAPHER: A. J. Hamler
ILLUSTRATOR: Jim Stack

ABOUT THE AUTHOR

A.J. Hamler is the former editor of *Woodshop News* and was the founding editor of *Woodcraft Magazine*. As a freelance writer, A.J.'s woodworking articles have appeared in most of the publications in the field and he recently served as Senior Editor for *The Collins Complete Woodworker* for HarperCollins/Smithsonian. When not in his workshop, his other interests include science fiction (writing as A.J. Austin, he's published two novels and numerous short stories), gourmet cooking and Civil War reenactments.

TABLE OF CONTENTS

Traditional Bluebird Box 16

Peterson Bluebird House 20

Finch House 26

Tree-Swallow House 30

Wood Duck House 34

Pipe Box 38

Wren House 42

Purple Martin Condo 46

Bat House 50

Butterfly House 54

Nesting Shelf 58

Chickadee House 62

3 feeding time 66

4 feathered fun 92

1

A BIT OF BIRD BUSINESS

When it comes to woodworking, birdhouses and feeders are among the most satisfying of projects. Unlike large endeavors, they don't require massive amounts of wood and don't take up much room during construction. Finishing methods are usually very simple (or can be dispensed with entirely). It doesn't take long to complete a birdhouse, making it the ideal weekend or evening projects. Best of all, once finished they're used and admired year-round.

This aim of this book is not to serve as an introduction to woodworking tools and techniques; I'll assume throughout the book that you have a general understanding of both. However, before we get to the projects themselves we should cover a few techniques and materials specific to birdhouses, with a special emphasis regarding construction for outdoor use.

CONSTRUCTION BASICS

Like all woodworking, building birdhouses is most successful with a good balance between tools and techniques. Let's look at both.

Because of their small size and minimal joinery, building birdhouses doesn't require a workshop full of state-of-the-art power equipment. Any of the projects contained here can be constructed with a basic kit of hand tools. A hammer, handsaw, hand drill, screwdriver, utility knife, a good square, straightedge and an assortment of sandpaper, combined with a selection of exterior-grade nails and screws are fine.

That said, a few power tools will certainly make things go more quickly and easily. The two most important and useful of these are a powered drill and saw.

Teamed with a good selection of bits (including spade or Forstner bits that excel at drilling entrance holes), a drill can produce accurate results quickly and reliably. A drill press, with its higher power and ability to make perfectly vertical holes, is even better.

A good jigsaw can handle a host of cutting chores, with crosscutting stock to length and ripping workpieces to width the most crucial. Further, a jigsaw's thin blade can easily cut curves and holes, and by adjusting the bottom of the jigsaw you can cut angles and bevels like a pro. Bench-top and stationary saws — table saw, band saw, scroll saw, etc. — add a large measure of accuracy and ease for turning out parts repetitively.

Rounding out the list of power tools for the birdhouse maker are nailers and sanders. Brad nailers, either electric or pneumatic, make for very fast work. Further, the thin nails they use have very small heads that aren't very visible in the finished projects. A hand sander is invaluable at providing perfectly smooth surfaces on just about any workpiece or finished project, while disc and spindle sanders excel at curved shapes.

There are no woodworking techniques specific to birdhouses; all methods used here are common throughout the workshop. However, a few things will pop up repeatedly.

Wood Grain

Grain direction is always a consideration in woodworking, but it's more important for exterior construction because wood exposed to the elements is prone to more stress than items produced for indoor use. Whenever possible, grain should always run in the direction of the longer dimension. Moisture can warp wood, and matching long grain with the longer dimension adds strength. It's also best to orient grain vertically whenever you can. Water runs vertically down a birdhouse when it rains, and is less likely to soak into wood if the grain also goes vertically. This is especially true of rough wood like cedar.

Although not always possible, try to orient end-grain away from flowing water. Likewise, when making joints strive to cover end-grain on upper parts of a project by overlapping long grain against it.

Doors and Access

Every birdhouse should have a way to open it. Because you'll occasionally want to observe a house's contents and occupants, and because all birdhouses require occasional cleaning, it must be possible to get inside. A dedicated door is the easiest method.

You can create a traditional door with weather-resistant hinges, and a few projects in this book (the most notably larger project like the wood duck house) use that method. However, access can also be designed right into the house by making one component moveable. The easiest way to do this is simply not attaching that component solidly. Instead, a single nail driven through each side of the components about and inch from one end creates a hinge. It's important to measure carefully when driving these two nails: If they're not set evenly and at the same distance on each side, the door will twist as it opens, or may not open smoothly at all. When a nail-hinge door is closed, you can secure it with a twisting toggle. A hook-and-eye arrangement like that on a screen door is another option, or you can simply drive in a single screw to keep it closed.

Be sure to place nails carefully to allow the door to open and close smoothly without twisting.

The other common method is to attach one component with screws — usually the floor or roof — so it can be removed for access.

Proper Drainage for Houses

Drainage is important to allow rainwater to exit the house. For houses with the floor inserted and attached between the house walls, the handiest method is to cut the corners off the floor. Or you can just drill a few holes through the floor; this method is best for birdhouses that use a base larger than the house itself.

Drainage holes serve a second purpose, in that they offer a bit of floor ventilation. We'll discuss general ventilation in a moment, but floor drainage allows air movement that helps to keep the nest dry even when collected rainwater isn't an issue.

Ventilation for Birdhouses

Birdhouses — especially those mounted in full sunshine — can get very hot. The entrance hole allows for some air movement, as do floor drainage holes. However, adding at least one hole near the top of the house where the hottest air collects helps keep nestlings comfortable.

For houses with traditional roof crowns, cutting the top ¼" to ½" off the crown of the rear wall works well, especially if the roof overhang helps block rainwater from getting in. For houses with doors, simply make the door slightly shorter than the door opening to create a small gap at the top that will allow for airflow.

If neither of these options is available in a particular house design, you can simply drill a few holes near the top of the house. It's best to locate these holes under an overhanging roof, but in any case drill these ventilation holes at an upward angle so rainwater isn't channeled inside.

Woodworking Safety

There's a safety warning posted at the front of this book, and I'd like to reinforce it here. You may notice that I've removed the guard on my table saw in some of the photography in the project chapters to make procedures easier to see, but I recommend you use all proper guards and safety equipment intended for your tools. Have adequate lighting in your work area at all times, and be sure to provide sufficient ventilation when working with glue, paint and stains. Above all, be sure to protect your eyes and ears.

There are a lot of sharp edges involved in woodworking, but one in particular seems to have popped up

Drainage is essential to keep the house interior dry. Notched corners or simple drilled holes will do the trick.

For houses kept in full sun all day, be sure to provide adequate ventilation.

only in recent years: staples. Because price stickers can fall off, home centers have taken to stapling price tags on the ends of lumber. Be absolutely certain to remove these before working with the lumber, as they can ruin blades if you inadvertently cut through them. If whoever put the staple there wasn't careful, one end of the staple may have missed the wood and be sticking out just waiting to skewer an unsuspecting finger. Even more distressing is the recent practice of applying multiple staples to wood edges. These are applied to "bridge" boards to keep them from sliding as they're stacked and shipped. The problem is that once the boards are separated one end of the staple comes out, resulting in dozens of sharp staple prongs sticking out of board edges. Be on the lookout for these when lumber shopping, and remove them immediately with pliers before working the lumber.

MATERIALS AND HARDWARE
Wood to Use

For natural-looking birdhouses, you probably want to leave the wood unfinished. For that reason, you'll need to choose your wood carefully. Softwoods, which are lighter and easier to work with than hardwoods, are the best choice. If a birdhouse needs repair, softwood components are usually easy to remove and replace. Cedar, redwood and cypress are among the most moisture-resistant softwoods you can find. They stand up well to the elements, and are resistant to both fungus and insect attack. All these wood species weather well, and all take on a silvery gray patina with exposure.

Although not quite as weather resistant, woods from the spruce/pine/fir families (usually referred to as SPF lumber) are also good choices, as is exterior-grade plywood. Houses made with these woods will last for years when left unfinished, but their useful lives will be extended considerably with paint or stain.

Hardwood lumber can make for bulletproof birdhouses, but hardwood can be difficult to work, especially with hand tools. Hardwood houses can be double (or more) the weight of a comparable house made with softwood. Among the hardwoods, teak is probably the best choice, but very expensive and not commonly available through local home centers. Oak, less expensive and more available, is another good hardwood choice.

Other woods, as well as plywood not rated for exterior use, may be considered for birdhouses, but should always be protected with paint or other finish.

Avoid wood with cracked edges or ends, oddly shaped grain, or obviously loose knots, and don't use treated lumber of any kind.

Glue, Nails and Screws

Not surprisingly, you should only use hardware that is resistant to the elements. For nails, galvanized are best. Likewise, galvanized, stainless steel, or coated exterior-grade or "deck" screws are preferable. Hinges, hooks, hangers, screw-eyes and other hardware should be of brass, stainless steel or other non-corrosive metals. Birdhouses should be examined periodically, and rusty hardware replaced as needed.

Paint and Stain

Any birdhouse can be painted or stained, however there are several things to keep in mind. First, use only exterior-grade paint, preferably a latex-based paint that is easier to use and cleans up with soap and water. Stick with lighter colors for birdhouses mounted in full sun; lighter colors reflect sunshine better, keeping the house interior a bit cooler. Reserve dark colors for houses place in protected areas, like on shaded tree trunks or in garden arbors, for example.

Use paint and stain only on exterior surfaces of a birdhouse or feeder. Fumes from the coatings (especially in hot weather), or chipping paint inside a house are potentially harmful to the inhabitants. When painting, avoid getting paint on the inside surface of the entrance holes, as that's a prime area where paint will chip free as birds come and go.

When painting wood requiring extra protection, it's important to cover all exposed surfaces to prevent water from getting into the wood itself. Filling nail holes and small gaps in joinery is a good idea before painting. This is especially important for plywood — even exterior-grade ply — that has voids, gaps or other openings

To avoid an unexpected cut, be wary of staples driven into board ends and edges. These must be removed before working the lumber with tools.

Typical birdhouse wood. Clockwise from lower left: Pine, cedar, red oak, exterior-grade plywood, "Baltic" birch plywood, birch-veneer plywood.

No matter what kind of plywood you use, edge voids allow water to get between the plies and speed up wood damage.

on the edges. Water will be attracted to these voids like a magnet, and the wood will be destroyed from the inside out. Fill these voids with a good-quality filler, and sand smooth before painting.

Any painted project for outdoors, particularly one made of plywood, will benefit from a coat of primer before painting. Priming seals the wood, especially edges and end grain, adding a layer of protection even before paint is applied. Priming also gives the wood a uniform color, helping paint cover evenly for the best appearance.

A good primer will help seal wood, especially plywood, helping it to better withstand the elements. As a bonus, priming improves paint adhesion and appearance.

HOUSE MOUNTING AND SUPPORT METHODS

If your birdhouse isn't likely to be disturbed by high wind or neighborhood predators (both two- and four-legged), you can simply hang them on hooks through a hole drilled in the back. For more security, drill mounting holes through the house back and screw them directly to a tree or post.

If you have overhead support, you can hang your birdhouse. Some of the house projects, like the Wren House and the Rocket, are designed to be suspended from screw eyes mounted in the tops of the houses.

Many birdhouses, and most feeders, work best when mounted a few feet off the ground out in the open. For these, a mount attached to the underside works best. Any store that carries bird supplies will have metal mounting brackets. These have a short pipe welded to a flat plate that can be screwed to the bottom of the house, allowing it to be slipped over a pole. If you can't find one of these mounts, two methods I've used are easy to make yourself. The plumbing department at your local home center sells copper end caps in a variety of sizes. Just drill a few holes in the bottom of the cap and screw it securely to the underside of the house, then select a mounting pole that fits snugly into the cap. You can also make a mounting block by gluing or nailing two rectangular pieces of wood together. Drill a large hole all the way through that matches the size of your mounting pole, then attach the block to the house with screws.

Houses can be pole-mounted a couple different ways. From left: A commercially available birdhouse mount, shop-made mounting block, copper plumbing end cap.

Odds and Ends

Finally, when it comes to decorating houses, be sure to check out your local craft supply store. They'll have a variety of hardwood dowels, discs, wheels and other components that can be adapted in dozens of ways.

Bird Specifics

Cavity-nesting birds have preferences and specific needs as it applies to house design and construction,

Craft supply stores carry a variety of hardwood and plywood components that can be used to decorate birdhouses. All should be primed and painted to withstand outdoor conditions.

and you'll find their requirements in the chart accompanying this section. Keep in mind that the specifications in the chart are guidelines only. Cavity-nesters are extremely adaptable, and very tolerant: If they find a spot they want for a nest, they couldn't care less that specs for the house they've picked are geared to another species. Essentially, if they can fit through the entrance and if there's enough room for the type of nest they build, it's home sweet home. I'll elaborate on this a bit in the headings that follow.

House Sizes

A cavity nester requires a specified minimum amount of space for nest construction and freedom of movement within the cavity. For best results in attracting specific birds you should stick closely to the guidelines listed in the chart when building houses, but you do have some wiggle room. For example, a wren needs a 4" × 4" space to call home. However, you can make this space narrower if you correspondingly increase the other dimension – no wren will turn up its beak at a house with a floor measuring 3½" × 5½". Likewise, adding extra inches to the minimum height listed on the chart will make little difference to prospective tenants.

Interior Considerations

Adult birds don't care what the inside of their houses look like, but nestlings must be able to climb out when the time comes. For that reason, the interior surface of the entrance wall should not be smooth. Some woods, like cedar, are very rough and simply orienting this rough face to the interior of the house suffices.

If the wood is smooth on both sides, you'll need to give the nestlings a little help with one of the methods used throughout this book. For a larger house like the Wood Duck House project, staple a piece of wire mesh inside the house beneath the entrance hole. Nestlings will use it like a ladder. For smaller houses, cut a series of shallow horizontal grooves below the entrance, or simply score the surface thoroughly with a utility knife or rotary tool.

Speaking of climbing, it may come as a surprise that no bird species needs a perch on the outside of the house. (In fact, only one project — the Wren House — includes a perch. Wrens do occasionally enjoy singing while on a perch, but they certainly don't need one.) Perches can also attract the wrong birds — house sparrows like them, for example — and can inadvertently help predators like cats and squirrels hang onto the house while reaching inside.

Finally, remember never to use paint, stain or any other kind of finish on the inside of your birdhouse.

Hole Size and Shape

The size of an entrance hole has two considerations: It must be large enough to admit the desired bird, yet small enough to discourage undesired birds. Holes also don't have to be round. Bluebirds and swallows rather like oval entrances more than other birds, so using an oval hole on a bluebird house may help to discourage undesired species. Other birds simply don't care what shape it is — if a wren can squeeze in, the hole can be round, square, triangular or even a thin slot.

If you're open to a couple types of birds using your birdhouse, choose a hole size in the middle of a range. To use wrens as an example again, they'll use holes from ⅞" to 1¼". That range (as well as a house sized for wrens) can also attract chickadees, creepers and titmice, so keep the hole on the small end of that range for wrens only.

The entrance heights listed on the chart are optimum heights, generally geared to be high enough to clear the top of the nest structure. You have some flexibility here when building houses, but again try to stay close to the recommended heights. Adjusting the entrance higher is always better than making it lower.

Location, Location, Location

As mentioned, birds are very tolerant and will often nest just about anywhere, but you have a better chance to getting the birds you want when taking a species' preferences into consideration in house mounting. First, stick closely to the mounting heights in the chart whenever possible. Likewise, there are little details that can make the difference in how readily a particular bird will move in. Bluebirds, for example, like to have a tree or other structure 20 to 30 feet directly in line with the front of their houses. I've given some of these mounting suggestions in the individual projects.

The important thing to keep in mind is terrain and landscaping. For example, you can have a perfect purple martin house mounted at exactly the right height, but even if martins are common in your region they won't go near your birdhouse if it's mounted in an area without a large open space or if the house is surrounded by lots of tall trees. Take local conditions into consideration when deciding what birdhouse you wish to put in your yard.

BIRDHOUSE CHART

SPECIES	FLOOR SIZE (IN.)	HOUSE HEIGHT (IN.)	ENTRY HOLE SIZE (IN.)	ENTRY HOLE HEIGHT (IN.)	MOUNTING HEIGHT (FT.)	NOTES AND COMMENTS
Bat	1¾ × 7½	23½	1 × 7½	Located on bottom	8-30	Dimensions here are specific to the project house; feel free to enlarge on bottom
Bluebird (Eastern)	5×5	8-12	1½	6-9	4-8	Oval hole should be 1⅜ × 2¼
Bluebird (Western & Mountain)	5×5	8-12	1-9/16	7-10	3-6	Oval hole should be 1⅜ × 2¼
Butterfly	3½ × 4½	16	½ × 3¼	n/a	2-5	Dimensions here are specific to the project house; feel free to enlarge
Cardinal	8×8	7-10	Open shelf	Open shelf	5-8	A nearby feeder will help attract cardinals to nest shelf
Chickadee (Black-Capped & Carolina)	4×4	8-12	1⅛	6-8	5-15	Floor dimensions shown are for square-sided house
Flicker	7×7	16-18	2½	14-16	6-20	A tree-mounted location is best
House Finch	6×6	6-7	2	4-6	8-12	Entry size may attract house sparrows
Kestrel (American)	6×6-8×9	9-15	3	9-12	12-30	Mount near open field with some trees or utility poles; add wood chips or other nest material; if mounted high on a barn, screech owls may move in
Mourning Dove	8×8	8-10	Open shelf	Open shelf	8-20	Dove nests are extremely loose, so a shelf enclosed by a low rail is best
Nuthatch (White-Breasted)	4×4	8-10	1¼	6-8	10-20	Wooded location is best
Nuthatch (Red-Breasted)	4×4	8-10	1¼	6-8	5-15	Extremely protective of nest, and will chase away other birds attracted to house, such as chickadees and even white-breasted nuthatches
Owl (Barn)	20×20	15-18	6	6	15-25	Entry hole can be round or 6×6 square
Owl (Screech)	8×8	12-16	3	9-12	15-30	Kestrels may also use this house if mounted in the open
Phoebe (Eastern)	7×7	6-8	Open shelf	Open shelf	8-12	Nest shelf may also attract robins
Prothonotary Warbler	5×5	6-8	1½	4-6	4-12	Mount near open water
Purple Martin	6×6	6	2-2¼	1-2	8-20	Mount in or adjacent to open field
Robin	7×8	7-9	Open shelf	Open shelf	6-12	Can be mounted near house window
Swallow (Barn)	6×6	6	Open shelf	Open shelf	8-12	Mount under roof or barn eaves
Swallow (Tree)	5×5	6-9	1½	4-6	4-10	Tree swallows often use bluebird boxes
Swallow (Violet-Green)	5×5	6-8	1½	4-6	5-15	
Wood Duck	9½×12	19-22	3×4	12-17	6-20	Entry hole is horizontal oval; floor size shown is minimal dimension; add wood chips or other nest material
Woodpecker (Downy)	4×4	8-10	1¼	6-8	5-20	Mount in partial to heavily wooded area
Woodpecker (Hairy)	6×6	12-15	1½	9-12	10-20	Mount in partial to heavily wooded area
Woodpecker (Red-Headed)	6×6	12-15	2	9-12	10-20	Mount in partial to heavily wooded area
Wren (House)	4×4	6-8	⅞ to 1⅛	4-6	4-10	Mount near bushes and low trees
Wren (Carolina)	4×4	6-8	1⅛	4-6	5-10	Mount near bushes and low trees
Wren (Bewick's)	4×4	6-8	1¼	4-6	4-12	Mount near bushes and low trees

THE WELCOME MAT: ATTRACTING BIRDS

This topic could easily fill its own book, but here are a few things to keep in mind if you want to make your yard a destination.

Trees and bushes are a must for most birds. Even birds like swallows and martins that feed in wide-open fields want trees for roosting, shelter and nesting. Species like woodpeckers, chickadees, nuthatches, wrens and flickers will rarely be seen in a treeless area. Evergreens can provide welcome shelter and protection both summer and winter.

Birds go where the food is. Birds that like nuts, berries and fruits will always be attracted to yards that have trees and bushes with these food sources. Carefully monitored feeders can draw birds to your yard where they'll find houses they might otherwise have missed. Even if your landscaping or terrain isn't suitable for nesting, you can often enjoy a lot of birds that may nest elsewhere but make a beeline for your yard for the free meal. Remember, too, that flowers attract a variety of insects, which are a tempting feast for insect-eating birds. Flowers also attract some fliers, like butterflies and hummingbirds, directly.

A source of water — such as a nearby pond or stream, a birdbath or even a goldfish pool — makes birds more likely to establish nests in an area. Take advantage of natural water sources, and consider providing water if there is none naturally.

Protect birds from predators. Fences will keep out dogs, along with most cats, raccoons and other large predators. When mounting houses and feeders, make it difficult for predators to get to them. Guards or baffles should be attached to pole-mounted structures to keep critters from climbing up. Hanging houses can have similar baffles installed above them.

Monitor your houses daily and evict any birds you don't want. If house sparrows try to move into your bluebird house before the bluebirds find it, or starlings decide they like your house finch birdhouse, kick 'em out! Open the houses frequently and destroy any nests-in-progress. Most undesirables give up fairly quickly and move on to easier pickings, making way for your desired tenants.

Winter Houses

Birds don't nest in winter, but that doesn't mean they won't spend a lot of time inside your birdhouses. So, don't be tempted to dismount your houses and put them away for the winter; check them frequently during colder months and clean them as needed; you'll frequently find evidence that birds have been spending nights huddled together inside or riding out particularly nasty storms.

Almost any house in this book will serve as a winter house, but you can also make houses specifically for winter. Just follow the general specs from the chart, but with a few differences. Even though the hole may be sized just right for a particular species, make the interior roomier. While it's generally one bird to a nest in the summer, up to a dozen birds of the same species may gather inside for warmth if there's room. On houses made for winter use, add drainage as usual but skip ventilation openings to cut down on drafts. Darker paint and stain choices for winter will help sunshine warm the interiors. For larger houses, consider adding an interior perch or two that runs the width of the house; this will help accommodate more birds.

And it almost goes without saying that you can make your birds happy all winter long with an adequate food supply, so keep your feeders well stocked every day.

No matter how nimble, no squirrel, raccoon or cat can climb past this pole-mounted guard.

Even though nesting season is long over, a birdhouse can be a warm refuge for birds all winter long.

Providing food is always a good way to attract birds, but supplying sustenance is even more important in the winter months.

2
ONE WITH NATURE

Many birdhouses work best when they blend in with their surroundings, becoming a natural part of the landscape.

Almost all of the houses presented here are unfinished, and use wood that weathers very well without further protection. For those houses that I've chosen to give some type of protective coating, you'll note that I've stuck closely to natural-looking stains and muted colors that blend well with their surroundings.

Most of these houses are species-specific, and are sized for particular birds. However, by using the chart in Part One as a guide, don't hesitate to alter the dimensions and entry holes to adapt them to other birds that may be common to your area.

traditional bluebird box

BLUEBIRDS ARE AMONG THE MOST-LOVED SPECIES in America, and for good reason: They're attractive, have a beautiful song, and earn their keep by eating lots of pesky insects. Organizations devoted to the bluebird are among the largest of all bird devotees, and when traveling around the country you're likely to see more bluebird houses along the roadsides than any other type.

While the newer design of the Peterson Bluebird Box in the next the chapter has proven very successful, bluebirds still love the more-familiar, standard square box that has been around for many years. By changing dimensions and other attributes, this basic design can be used as the basis for houses intended for many other species. In fact, the Swallow House project elsewhere in this book is of a similar design.

For this project, I've used guidelines from the North American Bluebird Society (NABS) (www.nabluebirdsociety.org) as my starting point, but made some changes to create a sturdier house. The house is made entirely of ¾" cedar.

Cut the house sides, top and floor to size, then cut ¼" – ⅜" off each corner of the floor as shown in the drawing for drainage/ventilation. Also go ahead and cut the front and back to length, but don't cut them to width yet. The sides, one of which will act as a lift-up door to access the interior, are angled at the top to match the roof slope of 10°, so a miter saw is the perfect tool to use when cutting the sides to length. (Fig. 1) You can also use a handsaw, or a table saw with a miter gauge, to make these cuts.

Now, why did I recommend waiting to cut the front and back to width? Off-the-shelf cedar — even though sold as ¾" thick — is often a bit thicker. That was the case with the stock I purchased for this house project; in fact, the ¾" cedar I got was ⅞", a full ⅛" thicker than its nominal thickness. Because this extra size can throw off dimensions, I opted to dry-assemble the house to check its exact width before cutting the front and back to width. Good thing I did, as the thicker sides

extended the width of the front and back by ¼" beyond the 5½" listed in the cut list for this project. As a result, you should always check the thickness of your stock – especially cedar – when sizing your components.

One easy way to make the adjustment is shown in Fig. 2. With my table saw unplugged, I've dry-assembled the floor and sides right against the blade, and then moved the fence in and locked it down. (Note the 5¾" adjusted width indicated by my steel rule.) Because the fence setting now matches the house width, when I cut the front and back to size, they'll be a perfect fit.

Both the front, back and roof are beveled to match the 10° roof slope, which I've elected to do on the table saw in Fig. 3. The front and back is beveled at the top, while the roof is beveled at the back. When cutting the bevel on the front, be sure to orient the bevel such that the rough side of the wood faces inward.

Drill a 1½" entrance hole through the front 6½" up from the bottom edge, as in Fig 4. The Forstner bit I'm using in Fig. 4 makes a very clean hole, but you can also use a hole saw. Place a piece of scrap beneath the workpiece to prevent tear-out on the back side. For safety, note that I've clamped the workpiece to the drill press table. In addition to the traditional round hole we're using here, bluebirds will also accept a 1⅜" × 2¼" oval hole, which I'll describe for the Peterson Bluebird Box in the next chapter. You can use either type for bluebird houses.

Using glue and nails, assemble the back, right side, front and floor, making sure that the beveled front and back align with the angled left side. The reason I've suggested to orient the front with the rough side in is to give nestlings an easier surface to climb when it's time to leave the nest. The cedar I used for this house was very rough, and it will work fine for the nestlings. However, if the cedar you get is particularly smooth on both sides, you may need to add some shallow cuts the nestlings can grab onto. I'll describe this alternative method in the next chapter.

Now, test-fit the left-side door, adjusting it with sandpaper or hand plane if it's too tight so that it will pivot easily. The left side is shorter than the right, and will leave a 1/4" ventilation gap at the top. With the bottom edge of the door even with the bottom of the house, measure about 7 1/2" up from the floor of the house and drive a galvanized nail through both the front and back of the house to act as hinges. (Fig. 5) Measure the nail locations exactly the same front and back so the door pivots properly. Drill a small hole 1" to 2" up from the bottom of the house and into the door edge and slip in a galvanized nail that will act as a lock to keep the door closed. Depending on how you plan to mount your house, you can drill this lock hole through either the front or back.

Finally, run a bead of glue along all the top edges, except the door, and nail the roof in place so the rear bevel is flush with the back.

The original NABS specifications for this house called for ventilation gaps on both sides of the house. However, that meant that the roof would be anchored on only the front and back of the house. I increased the height of the right side so it was flush with the underside of the roof, providing an additional attachment edge. Between the ventilation gap above the door, the entrance hole and the notches in the corners of the floor, this design offers plenty of fresh air circulation.

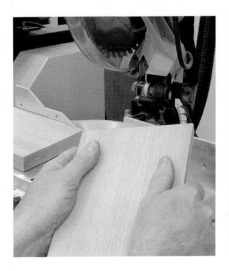

FIGURE 1 Either a miter saw, a handsaw or a table saw with a miter gauge can be used to cut the miters on the parts.

FIGURE 2 Here's an easy way to adjust the fence on your table saw for cutting the front and back parts to width.

FIGURE 3 The bevels on the top edges of the front, back and back of the top can be easily cut on the table saw.

FIGURE 4 A Forstner bit cuts a clean hole with smooth edges. You could also cut the hole using a hole saw.

FIGURE 5 Make sure the nails are the same distance from the bottom of the box so they function properly as hinges.

TRADITIONAL BLUEBIRD BOX • inches (millimeters)

REFERENCE	QUANTITY	PART	STOCK	THICKNESS	(mm)	WIDTH	(mm)	LENGTH	(mm)	COMMENTS
A	1	back	cedar	3/4	(19)	5 1/2	(140)	14 1/2	(368)	Length of back adjusted as needed for mounting.
B	1	front	cedar	3/4	(19)	5 1/2	(140)	9 3/8	(238)	
C	1	left side	cedar	3/4	(19)	5 1/2	(140)	10	(254)	
D	1	right side	cedar	3/4	(19)	5 1/2	(140)	10 1/4	(260)	
E	1	floor	cedar	3/4	(19)	5 1/2	(140)	4	(102)	
F	1	roof	cedar	3/4	(19)	8	(203)	10	(254)	

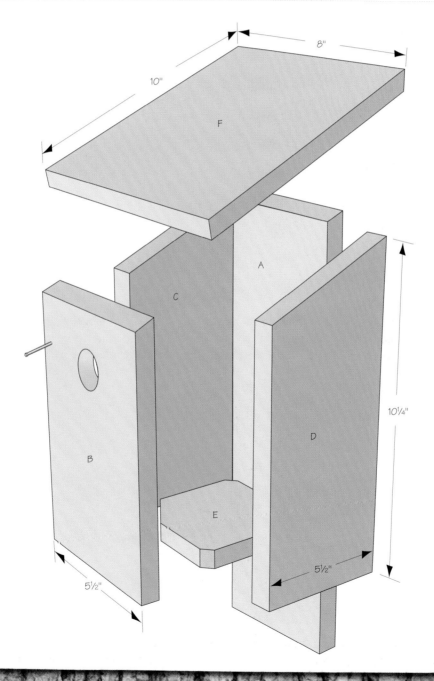

Peterson bluebird house

BACK IN THE 1970S, LONGTIME BLUEBIRD enthusiast Dick Peterson of Minnesota was concerned with declining bluebird populations in the Midwest. Hoping to encourage breeding, he spent years designing and testing a bluebird box radically different from the typical square house. Bluebirds loved the house's smaller floor area and oval entrance, and when an article on the birdhouse's success appeared in a Minneapolis newspaper, Peterson was so inundated with requests for plans that he turned to the Minneapolis Chapter of the National Audubon Society for help.

Working closely with the Society, he helped create the Bluebird Recovery Program of Minnesota, one of the largest statewide bluebird organizations in the country. The popularity of Peterson's birdhouse quickly spread to surrounding states, and to date tens of thousands have been made.

Begin by cutting the house components to size. For the birdhouse sides — the only components of the project not made up of plain rectangles — follow the pattern provided on the following page. I've used the band saw to cut out sides as in Fig. 1, but you can also use a jigsaw or handsaw. Follow your outlines carefully and use a sanding block or other sander to smooth your cuts if necessary. All other components can be cut on the table saw, which will give you perfectly straight cuts,

Because Dick Peterson intended his birdhouses to be erected by the hundreds across the countryside — and to remain there for many years — he designed the house to use a standard 2×4 as the main structure for superior strength. I've followed his design closely here, but will describe a variation on this at the end of the chapter.

With a 2×4 as the backbone of the structure, it can also serve as the post; simply use a full-length 2×4 and plant the lower end in the ground. A standard 2×4 used this way won't last forever when in contact with the ground, but a couple good coats of exterior stain or other sealant on the lower portion before planting will help it last for years. (Do not use a treated 2×4 for this project however, as the bluebirds will come into contact with it in the box interior.)

The tops of the birdhouse sides slope down, so to make the roof match this angle, cut the 7³⁄₈" inner roof from the end of your 2×4 at a 63° angle on the table saw. When you turn this piece over and attach it to the top of the beveled 2×4, the two 63° angles will form the slope of the roof. With the saw still set at 63°, flip your 2×4 around and cut the 3"-long floor off the other end. The floor will meet the front of the birdhouse at a right angle, so leave the end of this piece square, but reset the saw blade to 45° and cut a bevel on the square end of the inner roof. This will help form a ventilation gap at the top of the house, which I'll describe shortly.

Put a bit of waterproof glue on the 63° end of the inner roof and toe-nail it in place against the top bevel of the 2×4. Now, measure down 9" from the underside of the roof and mark the 2×4 for the location of the floor. Apply a bit of glue to the floor, line the top of the piece with the line and toe-nail it in place as in Fig. 2.

Apply glue to the edges of the 2×4 house structure, and nail each side in place (Fig. 3).

Cut a 45° bevel on the top of the birdhouse door/front. Draw a short centerline down from the top and use a compass to draw a 1³⁄₈" circle on your line about 1" from the top, as in Fig. 4. Overlap a second circle to create a 2¼" oval. Cut out this oval hole, then sand the hole edges smooth. A spindle sander or a sanding drum on the drill press works well for this.

Nestlings sometimes find it difficult to climb out of a birdhouse when it's time to leave the nest, so cut some very shallow grooves into the inner surface of the door/front about ½" to ¾" apart. These cuts can be done on the table saw as in Fig. 5, or with a handsaw. As you can see in Fig. 6, these cuts don't have to be very deep at all; just a light scoring is plenty to give the nestlings' little claws a good foothold for climbing.

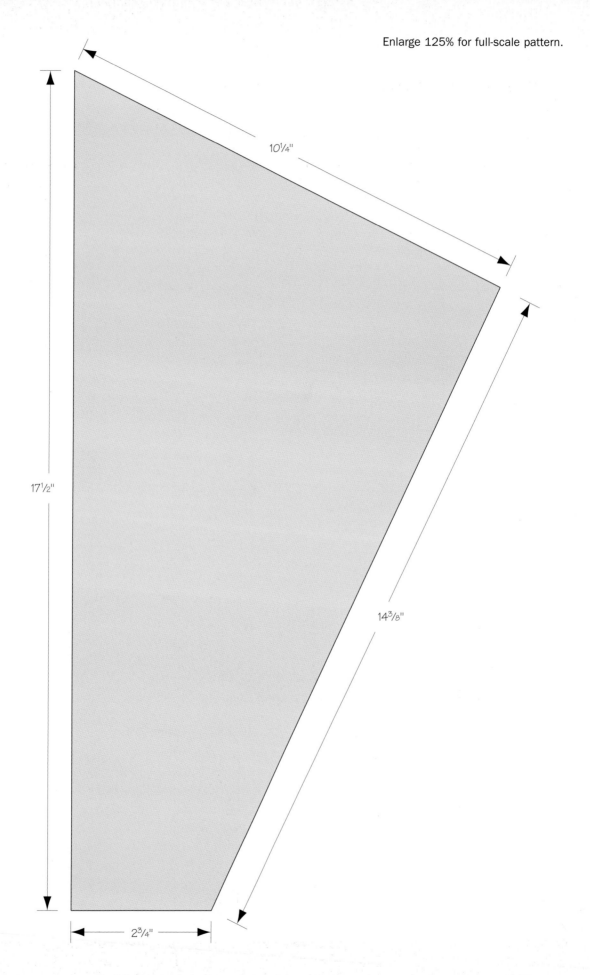

Enlarge 125% for full-scale pattern.

10¼"

17½"

14³⁄₈"

2¾"

PETERSON BLUEBIRD HOUSE • inches (millimeters)

REFERENCE	QUANTITY	PART	STOCK	THICKNESS	(mm)	WIDTH	(mm)	LENGTH	(mm)	COMMENTS
A	1	main post/back	2×4	$1^1/_2$	(38)	$3^1/_2$	(89)			length as needed for mounting the box
B	1	interior roof	2×4	$1^1/_2$	(38)	$3^1/_2$	(89)	$7^3/_8$	(187)	
C	1	bottom	2×4	$1^1/_2$	(38)	$3^1/_2$	(89)	3	(76)	
D	2	sides	cedar	$3/_4$	(19)	$10^1/_4$	(89)	$17^1/_2$	(446)	
E	1	roof	cedar	$3/_4$	(19)	9	(229)	13	(330)	
F	1	bottom	cedar	$3/_4$	(19)	$3^1/_2$	(89)	$12^1/_2$	(318)	

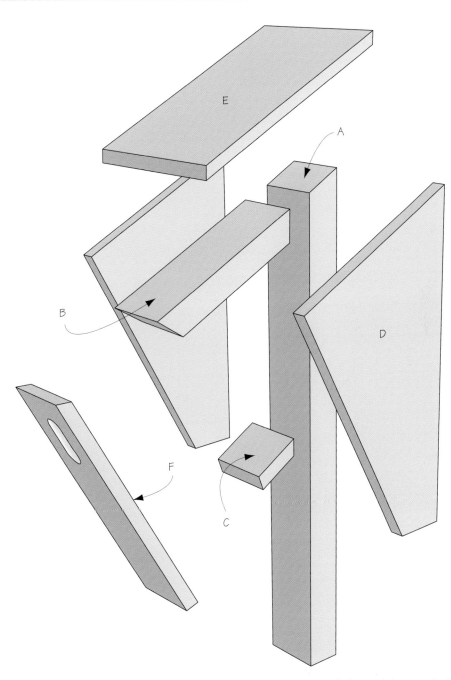

Test fit the door/front, and sand or plane the sides so it's not too tight; it will need to pivot smoothly. Hold the front so that it leaves a ½" to ⅝" gap at the top, and you'll note how the 45° angled cuts on the inner roof and door/front create an even gap for ventilation. Drive a 2" galvanized finish nail through each side so that it anchors into the door/front about 1" up from the bottom of piece (Fig. 7). Because this will be a pivot hinge, it's best to measure and mark this to ensure that the nails are set exactly the same on each side; otherwise, it won't function properly as a drop-down door. Drill a hole 6" or 7" up from the pivot nail on one side to slip in a galvanized nail that will act as a lock to keep the door/front in the upright position. To open the drop-down door, just remove the nail.

Finally, drill ¼" or ⅜" ventilation holes at the top rear on each side of the house.

If you've opted to use a full-length 2×4 as the main post, you have plenty of length left after cutting off the inner roof and floor pieces to plant the end in the ground. Dig a hole deep enough so the house's entrance hole is about 5' off the ground. If possible, angle the house so that it faces a nearby tree or fence; bluebirds like to monitor the area in front of their home.

Now, if you'd prefer to use some other mounting method, use a 24"-30" length of 2×4 for the back of the house. The house can be mounted by drilling a pair of screw or bolt holes in the lower portion of the 2×4, or with one hole drilled through the lower portion and a second drilled through the back of the house (attach with a screw or bolt from inside the house with the door lowered). Using a 2×4 in this way will ensure the strength that Dick Peterson intended for his house.

If you don't need the extra strength or you'd just prefer a lighter birdhouse, simply use the same ¾" stock for the back and floor as you did for the rest of the house, and eliminate the inner roof. Adjust the dimensions of the two sides accordingly to keep the interior dimensions of the box the same.

FIGURE 1 I've used the band saw to cut out sides, but you can also use a jigsaw or handsaw.

FIGURE 2 Apply a bit of glue to the floor, line the top of the piece with the line and toe-nail it in place.

FIGURE 3 Apply glue to the edges of the 2×4 house structure, and nail each side in place.

FIGURE 4 Draw a short centerline down from the top and use a compass to draw a 1⅜" circle on your line about 1" from the top. Overlap a second circle to create a 2¼" oval.

FIGURE 5 Cut some very shallow grooves into the inner surface of the door/front.

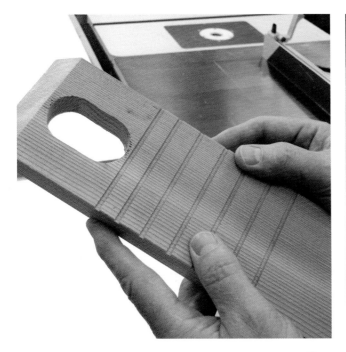

FIGURE 6 A light scoring is plenty to give the nestlings' little claws a good foothold for climbing.

FIGURE 7 Because this will be a pivot hinge, it's best to measure and mark so the nails are set exactly the same on each side; otherwise, it won't function properly as a drop-down door.

finch house

OF THE MORE THAN TWO-DOZEN BIRDHOUSES and feeders in this book, not many have the traditional shape of a real house. This House Finch project — along with the Cottage House in a later chapter — is one of the exceptions. Made entirely of ¾" cedar, it features a two-sided roof with a 90° crown that gives it an attractively sloped profile.

Cut the house components to size, paying particular attention to the necessary angles and bevels for the roof. To create a house with a 90° crown, the house sides are beveled at 45° at the top, while the front and back components are cut to a tapered point at 45° angles on each side.

As you work your way through the projects, you'll learn that I'm a big fan of cutting multiple components at the same time whenever possible. It not only saves time, but it assures that your angles are identical when cutting pieces in matching pairs. After marking the cut lines for the workpieces for the front and back of the house, drive a short screw through the entry hole location to hold the two pieces together. (For house finches, an entry hole located 4"-6" on-center above the floor works well.) A few brads in waste areas of the workpiece are also a good idea as you cut the two pieces simultaneously. (Fig. 1).

Remove the screw to separate the two pieces, then drill a 2" entry hole in the front piece where the screw was. It's very easy to create ventilation for this house simply by cutting ½" off the pointed top of the back workpiece piece before assembling the house.

Begin the assembly by deciding which side of the house will act as the door and which side will be fixed. I've chosen the right side as the door here, but you can use either one. With nails and waterproof glue, attach the front and back of the house to the fixed side, taking care that the beveled top of the side is even with the angled edges of the front and back. Now cut ¼" to ⅜" off each corner of the floor to create drainage and slip it into place, securing it with nails as in Fig. 2.

Flip the house on end and put the door side in place. Drive galvanized nails through each side to act as hinges for the door. Be sure the nail locations are the same both front and back, or the door won't pivot correctly. In Fig. 3 I'm using a nail set to tap the hinge nails just below the surface.

Starting with the shorter of the two roof sides, apply a bit of glue to the angled edges of the front and back, align the roof carefully and nail it into place. (I've located the short roof side on the left on this house, but it doesn't matter which side you put it on.) Now put some glue on the angled edges on the other side — as well as on the roof edge as in Fig. 4 — and nail the longer roof side in place.

Finally, add a twist latch. I've rounded the edges of a ¾" × ¾" × 2¼" piece of cedar and screwed it to the house near the bottom of the side door. Tighten the screw enough to keep the latch securely in place, but still easy to twist to the side when accessing the inside of the house for cleaning.

House finches like their nests on the high side, so mount your completed finch house on a tree or tall post between 8' and 12' above the ground. Be aware that the large 2" hole may invite less desirable house sparrows and starlings, so you may have to do some eviction duties to keep it vacant until house finches move in.

FIGURE 1 Attach the front and back pieces together and cut them at the same time.

FIGURE 2 Nail the sides to the floor.

FIGURE 3 Be sure the nail locations are the same both front and back, or the door won't pivot correctly.

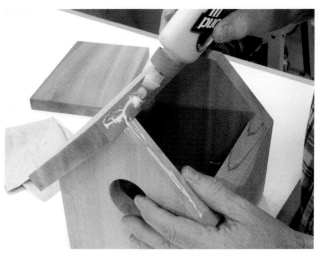

FIGURE 4 Attach the short roof side first, the nail the longer roof side in place

a note about house finches

Common throughout the U.S. and Mexico, house finches resemble a large house sparrow, but with a dash of color and a delightful song. Both sexes are streaked with shades of brown and gray, but the male blends to red toward the head and breast. They like populated areas and are comfortable in close quarters with humans. Strictly vegetarians, house finches are frequent visitors to feeders stocked with thistle seeds. Because they're year-round residents, they appreciate feeders during the winter in colder climates.

FINCH HOUSE • inches (millimeters)

REFERENCE	QUANTITY	PART	STOCK	THICKNESS	(mm)	WIDTH	(mm)	LENGTH	(mm)	COMMENTS
A	2	front/back	cedar	$^3/_4$	19	7	178	$8^1/_4$	209	
B	2	sides	cedar	$^3/_4$	19	$5^1/_2$	140	$6^1/_2$	165	
C	1	left roof	cedar	$^3/_4$	19	$5^1/_2$	140	$9^1/_4$	235	
D	1	right roof	cedar	$^3/_4$	19	$6^1/_4$	159	$9^1/_4$	235	
E	1	floor	cedar	$^3/_4$	19	$5^1/_2$	140	$6^1/_2$	165	
F	1	twist latch	cedar	$^3/_4$	19	$^3/_4$	19	$2^1/_4$	57	

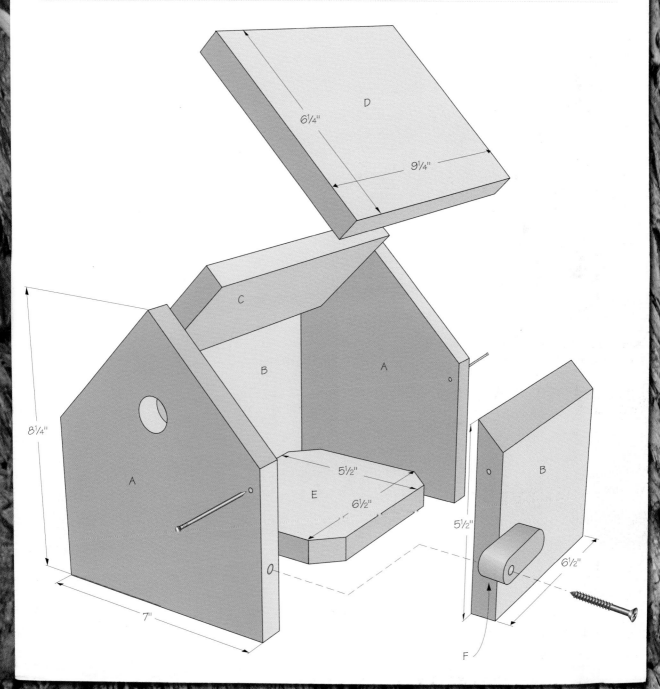

tree-swallow house

I MENTIONED IN AN EARLIER CHAPTER THAT the Traditional Bluebird Box is of such a basic design, that with a few changes in overall dimensions and entry-hole size, one could easily be the template for a variety of bird homes. That's the case with the design for this swallow house.

Although swallows will happily live in a larger house (I've occasionally had them move into the somewhat larger bluebird box on my property), they don't need quite as much room as bluebirds. Still, the basic design is very similar, just scaled down a bit. Also, where the bluebird box used a roof wider than the house itself, the roof on this swallow house is the same width as the other components, allowing all the parts to be cut from a single piece of 1×6 cedar.

Because this house is so similar to the one for bluebirds, it uses the same components. And, since the assembly process proceeds in the same order, I won't repeat many of the assembly photos here.

Lay out your parts on the stock, noting in Fig. 1 how I've worked around a particularly large open knothole. Knots are fine in birdhouses — and can even lend an attractive touch — but open holes should be avoided unless they're very small. With luck and some careful stock layout, you may be able to have these open knots fall in strategic spots, such as where the entry, drainage or ventilation holes will be.

You may have noticed that for this box, I've opted to have the door on the right side of the house instead of on the left as with the Bluebird Box. It doesn't matter which side you choose for the door; just remember that the door side is ¼" shorter to create a ventilation gap at the top.

Cut out the house sides, roof and floor to size, angling the tops of each side and beveling the back edge of the roof by 10° for the roof slope. As with the bluebird house, create drainage holes by cutting ¼" - ⅜" off the corners of the floor. Also go ahead and cut the front and back to length and bevel the top edge of

the front at 10° for the roof slope, orienting the bevel so the rough face of the house front faces in. Don't cut the front and back to width yet. Because of the variances in cedar thickness, you'll want to take do a dry assembly of the house and take actual measurements of the front and back for a perfect fit using the method described in the Traditional Bluebird Box project. Once you've made these measurements, cut the front and back to accommodate the exact house width. (If your cedar is a true ¾" thick, you won't need to make this adjustment.)

Drill a 1½" entrance hole through the front 6" up from the bottom edge and sand the rim of the hole if needed to remove any sharp edges. Examine the inner surface of the front carefully; you should have oriented this part with the rough side in, and if the face of the cedar is good and rough there's no need to do anything further. If it's unusually smooth, however, add some grooves to assist the nestlings when it's time for them to climb out. Attach the front to the left side of the house with glue and nails, making sure the top bevel aligns with the side roof angle. Now attach the front/side assembly to the house back, centering it vertically. This will allow you drill mounting holes in the back both above and below the house. Note in Fig. 2 that I'm using the right side of the house as a temporary support spacer to make nailing on the back a bit easier.

Nail the floor into place, even with the bottom edges of the side and front. Test-fit the right-side door and adjust as necessary with sandpaper or hand plane if it's too tight. With the bottom edge of the door even with the bottom of the house, measure about 7" up and drive a galvanized nail through the front and the corresponding point on the back of the house to act as hinges. With the main portion of the house assembled, nail the roof in place so that the rear bevel is flush with the back, as in Fig. 3. Be sure not to use glue or nails on the side where the door is.

Remember that unusable piece of wood left over with the large knothole? Well, I'm one of those woodworkers who don't believe in scrap, so I hung onto that small piece. Some of the projects with lift-up doors utilize a galvanized nail slipped into a hole to keep the door closed. As with the Finch House project, I cut a ¾" × ¾" × 2¼" section from that piece that will function as a twist latch to secure the door. You can use this piece as-is, but I rounded each end on the disc sander.

Drill a pilot hole through this piece and one edge of the house front about an inch or two up from the bottom, then attach this latch with a screw. Screw this to the side of the house just tightly enough that the latch stays where you put it; don't over tighten. Once the house is mounted, you can just twist this latch to the side to free the door.

FIGURE 1 Layout the parts to use the best parts of the board.

FIGURE 2 I'm using the right side of the house as a temporary support spacer

FIGURE 3 Nail the roof in place so that the rear bevel is flush with the back.

FIGURE 4 Don't over tighten the screw that holds the twist latch in place. It should turn easily.

TREE-SWALLOW HOUSE • inches (millimeters)

REFERENCE	QUANTITY	PART	STOCK	THICKNESS	(mm)	WIDTH	(mm)	LENGTH	(mm)	COMMENTS
A	1	back	cedar	3/4	19	5 1/2	140	15	381	
B	1	front	cedar	3/4	19	5 1/2	140	8	203	
C	1	right side	cedar	3/4	19	5 1/2	140	8 3/4	222	
D	1	left side	cedar	3/4	19	5 1/2	140	9	229	
E	1	floor	cedar	3/4	19	5 1/2	140	4	102	
F	1	roof	cedar	3/4	19	5 1/2	140	8	203	
G	1	twist latch	cedar	3/4	19	3/4	19	2 1/4	57	

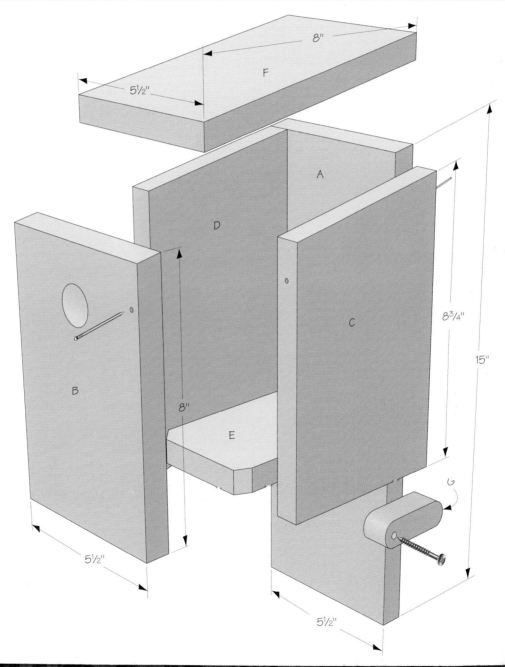

wood duck house

YOU RARELY SEE DUCKS IN TREES, AND YOU'LL see even fewer nesting in cavities there. The beautiful wood duck, found in all but the most arid regions of the U.S. and Mexico, is one of those few exceptions. And because they're cavity nesters, they readily welcome well-built houses in their habitats.

This painted house is made of a mix of solid pine and plywood, but cedar or another wood species would be fine if you prefer an unfinished house. Access for cleaning and maintenance is through a hinged plywood roof.

Cut all house components to size, angling the tops of each side 10° for the roof slope, and bevel the top edges of the front and back by the same amount. Note that the left side of the house is ¾" shorter than the right, allowing for plenty of ventilation on hot days.

Mark the outline for the 3" × 4" oval entrance hole on the front, 3½" below the top edge, measured at the hole's center. Clamp the front to a workbench or other secure work surface, and drill a ½" hole somewhere on the inside edge of the oval. Slip the blade of a jigsaw into this hole and cut out the opening as in Fig. 1.

Mother wood ducks don't offer any help for their nestlings to get out of the house when they're old enough to leave the nest, which is only a day or two after hatching. In fact, when it's time for them to leave the nest, she sits out on the water and calls for them to jump out, so they'll need some assistance climbing to the entrance. Use a pair of snips or diagonal cutters to make a 6" × 12" rectangle of wire mesh, which they can use as a ladder. Cut the edges of the mesh as closely as possible, and maybe even run a sanding block or file around the edges to remove any sharp wire spurs left from cutting. Staple this mesh ladder to the inner surface of the house front just below the entrance hole, as in Fig. 2. Take care that the bottom of the mesh is at least ¾" above the bottom edge of the workpiece so it doesn't interfere with installing the floor.

Assemble the front, sides and back of the house with waterproof glue and nails. Drill six evenly spaced ¼" drainage holes through the floor, then slip it into the bottom of the house and nail securely in place.

Your duck house can be mounted on a tree or pole, but because it's a heavy house I recommend using lag screws or bolts for the job. Make a center line on the back of the house and drill a pair of holes to accept a couple of these fasteners, as in Fig. 4.

Finally, install the roof. Flip the house upside down onto the roof, and use a 10" continuous hinge (sometimes called a piano hinge) to attach the house to roof about 1" from the roof's rear edge as in Fig. 5. Continuous hinges are usually sold in minimum lengths of 24", so you'll probably need to cut this hinge to length; a hacksaw or rotary tool with a cutting disc make quick work of this task. Even though the plywood roof is hefty, a strong wind — or the average raccoon — will be able to flip it open easily. Drill a pilot hole through the roof and down into the house front, and keep the lid closed with a screw that can be removed to open the house for cleaning.

Paint the house with an exterior latex or enamel paint, but stick to white or light pastel colors to reflect summer heat. Do not paint inside the house or the underside portion of the roof that is inside the house; the underside of the roof eaves is fine. Protect the inner edge of the entrance hole with masking tape while painting.

Your Wood Duck house should be mounted on a tree or pole as close to the water as you can, or even out in the water if possible. Use a sturdy pole long enough that the house will be a minimum of 4' above the highest anticipated water level, with the front of the house facing the water. Be sure to orient the front of the house so there are no branches or other obstacles in a flight path to the entrance hole.

Before mounting, toss a few inches of wood shavings into the house, since wood ducks don't collect material to build nests. Sawdust is too fine and granular to use and should be avoided, but planer or jointer chips are excellent choices.

FIGURE 1 Make the cutout for the entrance hole. Use a drilled hole to get started cutting.

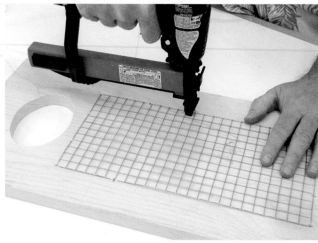

FIGURE 2 Attach the wire mesh using staples. Be sure the edges of the mesh are smooth.

FIGURE 3 Use waterproof glue and nails to assemble the box.

FIGURE 4 Use lag screws or bolts, driven through the back of the box, to attach the box to a pole or tree.

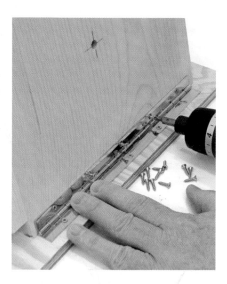

FIGURE 5 To attach the continuous hinge to the top, turn the box upside down and simply hold the hinge in place and install the screws.

a note about wood ducks

Wood ducks are among the most beautiful ducks around, especially the male with its red eyes and mix of white, yellow/gold, tan and iridescent black, green, blue and purple. Females are more plainly colored in shades of gray/brown, tan and white, with blue on the wings. Both sexes sport down-swept head crests. Wood ducks are the only North American duck that has two broods a year; a good thing, as they are the second-most hunted duck in the U.S., after mallards.

Image copyright Bryan Brazil, 2009. Used under license from Shutterstock.com.

WOOD DUCK HOUSE • inches (millimeters)

REFERENCE	QUANTITY	PART	STOCK	THICKNESS	(mm)	WIDTH	(mm)	LENGTH	(mm)	COMMENTS
A	1	front	pine	3/4	19	10	254	19	483	
B	1	left side	pine	3/4	19	11	279	20 1/4	514	
C	1	right side	pine	3/4	19	11	279	21	533	
D	1	back	pine	3/4	19	10	254	21	533	
E	1	floor	pine	3/4	19	9 1/2	241	10	254	
F	1	roof	plywood	1/2	13	14	356	14	356	
G	1	1/2" wire mesh	galvanized			6	152	12	305	
H	1	continuous hinge	brass					10	254	any non-corrosive hinge may be used

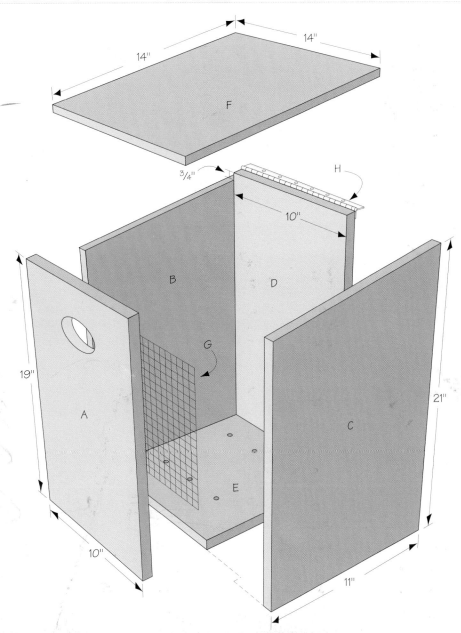

pipe box

UP TO THIS POINT, WE'VE USED CEDAR AND other natural materials for these projects. However, PVC pipe can also be used to make a birdhouse with minimal construction. Not only can PVC houses be made quickly — a boon if your goal is to install numerous birdhouses around a large property with a lot of acreage — but PVC houses are extremely resistant to weather. In fact, they're nearly indestructible.

PVC is available in a variety of diameters, but stick with either 4" or 6" pipe. PVC comes in different formulations depending on their intended use in home construction, but I've found that foam-core PVC is the best to work with for birdhouses. It's very light, and although the inner and outer surfaces are hard, the interior is soft foam as the name implies. Also, while PVC usually comes in minimum 8' lengths, home centers often sell foam-core PVC pipe in shorter 24" pieces, meaning you don't have to buy full lengths.

I've sized this pipe house for bluebirds, and although most bluebird boxes are at least 4½" × 4½" on the inside, I've found that they'll eagerly use a house based on 4" pipe. To offer a bit more room for nest material, I've raised the height of the entry hole a bit over that of a traditional bluebird box. Of course, PVC pipe can be adapted to just about any bird by adjusting the size of pipe used and the entry-hole size.

Start by cutting your pipe to length. This can be done with a jigsaw or band saw, but cutting a round object of this size can be cumbersome with power tools, so if you have any doubts, use a hand saw only. *Never attempt to cut PVC pipe on a table saw.* Fortunately, you'll find that foam-core PVC cuts very easily by hand, as shown in Fig. 1. Naturally, I'm cutting the pipe at a 10° angle to maintain my preferred roof slope. You can use a steeper angle if you'd like, or none at all. Note in Fig. 1 how I've opened my bench vise a few inches and rested the pipe in it for support as I cut. The vise jaws aren't tight against the pipe, but the pipe nestles securely in the gap. I recommend supporting PVC pipe in this or a

similar manner for both safety and to make it easier to work with.

All PVC pipe is printed with a variety of information — type, company names, usage warnings, etc. — but this printing is easily removed with mineral spirits or alcohol. (Fig. 2.) Once you've removed the markings, follow with a clean rag dampened with plain water to remove any residual alcohol. When you have the pipe clean, use a dark pencil to note the front of the house – because the house is perfectly round, this will help keep the orientation correct for the following steps.

PVC is very smooth, which can make it difficult for nestlings to scramble out when it's time. So, lightly score the inside of the PVC on what will be the front of the house as in Fig. 3. A rotary tool is perfect for this. You'll only need to make the scoring a few inches long, and only up to the entry hole, which will be located in a later step.

Trace a 4" circle onto a piece of ¾" pine or other wood, and cut the disc out with a jigsaw or band saw, then sand as needed so that if fits inside the pipe. (If you plan to make several of these homes, it'll be helpful to cut a 1" slice of pipe to keep on hand for tracing purposes.) Since this disc will be the floor, drill a few ¼" drainage holes in it. Drill three countersunk pilot holes evenly spaced around the bottom of the pipe, and screw the floor into place with 1¼" exterior-grade wood screws as in Fig. 4. This way you can remove and easily replace the floor as needed to clean out the house. *By the way, PVC can melt when machined at high speed, so keep the speed low if you're using a variable-speed drill.*

Drill a 1½"-diameter entry hole on the front of the house 8" up from the bottom. Note in Fig. 5 that I'm supporting the pipe by cradling it in a wooden miter box, which in turn rests securely on my drill press table. Again, adjust the drill press to a lower speed (if you can) to prevent melting the PVC.

Before attaching the roof you'll need another 4" disc insert, and to accommodate the roof slope it should be thicker. I cut mine from a scrap of standard pine 2×6, which gives a disc 1½" thick. Insert the disc in the top of the pipe and secure in place. You can use screws again, but I used the same nailer I've been using for all these projects — foam-core PVC is easily nailed.

When the upper disc is firmly in place, cut it at an angle to match the top of the pipe. Apply a bit of glue to the disc, then nail the roof in place as in Fig. 6. Finally, drill ¼" or ⅜" ventilation holes at the top on each side of the house.

You can leave your pipe house as is — the bright white is a perfect color to reflect the hot sun — or you can paint the pipe if you wish. Rough up the PVC a bit with sandpaper before painting and apply a good-quality exterior primer, followed by the exterior latex paint of your choice. As always, avoid getting paint on the interior of the entry hole.

FIGURE 1 My vise acts as a third hand to help steady the PVC while I cut it.

FIGURE 2 Remove the printing on the pipe using solvent.

FIGURE 3 Score the inside of the pipe to create footholds for the nestlings.

FIGURE 4 Pre-drill the pipe using a drill bit with a countersink. Attach the floor to the pipe with 1¼" exterior screws.

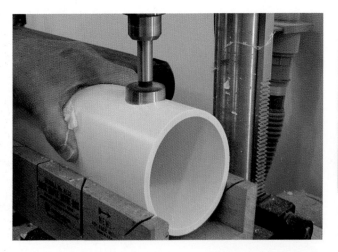

FIGURE 5 Use a miter box or make a cradle to hold the pipe. Using the lowest speed on your drill press, cut the 1½"-diameter entrance hole.

FIGURE 6 Nail the roof to the upper disc.

PIPE BOX • inches (millimeters)

REFERENCE	QUANTITY	PART	STOCK	THICKNESS	(mm)	WIDTH	(mm)	LENGTH	(mm)	COMMENTS
A	1	pipe	Foam-core PVC			4d	102	11	279	
B	1	floor	pine	³⁄₄	19	4d	102			
C	1	roof insert	pine	1¹⁄₂	38	4d	102			
E	1	roof	cedar	³⁄₄	19	7	178	8	203	

wren house

IF BLUEBIRDS ARE THE SYMBOL OF HAPPINESS, then surely wrens represent comedy. These busy little birds hop and flit everywhere, with many of their movements almost too fast to detect. Their stooped posture and raised tails are distinctive, and their songs particularly bubbly in nature. Although not the most colorful of birds, they are strikingly beautiful nonetheless.

As I noted in Part One, many birds aren't fussy when it comes to choosing a home in spite of our best efforts to make houses perfect for a particular species. House sparrows and starlings aren't picky at all, although they're not particularly welcome either. Wrens, on the other hand, are among the most desirable and one of the least fussy of all songbirds. They'll almost literally nest in any box or cavity – nail a tennis shoe to a tree and don't be surprised to see a wren move in.

The house in this project with its 1⅛" entrance hole is appropriate for the house wren, as well as the Carolina wren (eastern U.S.) and Bewick's Wren (western and south-central U.S. and Mexico). Don't be surprised if chickadees are attracted to it as well. If you prefer to attract only house wrens, decrease the entrance hole to ⅞", about the size of a United States quarter.

I've opted to use ½" plywood and spray paint it when completed. You can use any untreated wood however, painted or left natural. The angles of some of the components may seem daunting at first, but using the pattern on page 45 simplifies things.

Begin by transferring the pattern outline for the front/back workpieces. This is easiest to do by placing the pattern on the workpiece and simply piercing the pattern corners with an awl, nail or other sharp instrument as shown in Fig. 1, and then connect the dots. To make cutting easier and to assure two identical components, rough-cut the pattern and sandwich it on top of a second rough-cut workpiece. Drive screws through the workpiece corners, plus one through the entrance location to hold the two pieces together, then cut them at the same time, as in Fig. 2. Cut just up to the lines on the four longest sides, but don't cut the top line yet. With the two workpieces still joined, clean up your four cuts on a disc sander or with a sanding block. Now make the final cut and, carefully avoiding twisting the two workpieces on the remaining screw at the entrance hole location, sand the last side. (Fig. 3) Remove the final screw, and mark the two inside faces to keep the orientation correct. This will assure a perfect fit for the other components, plus will keep the screw hole in the back toward the inside of the house. Drill a 1⅛" hole in the front as indicated on the pattern.

Cut the remaining components, beveling the joining edges at 67.5° to match the 112.5° angle of the corners on the front/back. (The bottom corner of the front/back is 90°, so no bevel is needed there.)

Attach the two lower sides to the front/back components with glue and nails, then follow with the left and right roof sections as in Fig. 4 or with a handsaw. For cleaning purposes we'll make the top removable, so attach it with screws only. Drill countersunk pilot holes through the top and into the front/back components, taking care to avoid both the entrance hole and any nails you used.

As noted in Part One, it's fine to paint any birdhouse as long as the paint is confined to the exterior only. Don't paint the inner edges of the entrance hole. In Fig. 5 I'm using spray paint for a fast finishing job.

When the paint has dried, drill two ¼" holes near the bottom point for drainage, one ¼" hole beneath each roof eave for ventilation, and one ¼" hole for the perch 1" below the house entrance (don't drill this last hole all the way through). Glue the perch in place, but do not paint it.

Your wren house can be mounted on a pole or tree trunk, or can be hung. For the hanging version shown here, screw a pair of screw eyes into the top of the house and hang with heavy twine or leather strips.

FIGURE 1 Use the pattern on page 45 and lay out the front and back.

FIGURE 2 Cut the front and back parts at the same time to ensure that they are the same size and shape.

FIGURE 3 Sand the saw cuts.

FIGURE 4 Attach the two lower sides to the front/back components with glue and nails, then follow with the left and right roof sections.

FIGURE 5 Paint only the outside of the house. That includes masking off the sides of the entrance hole so no paint gets on them.

a note about wrens

Colored in various patterns and shades of brown, wrens are among the most active and animated of birds — they rarely hold still. They're found throughout the Western Hemisphere, with the house wren the most common in the U.S. They're fiercely territorial and will chase off any birds, including larger birds and other wrens, if they feel threatened. They subsist almost entirely on insects and migrate to warmer climates in the winter.

WREN HOUSE • inches (millimeters)

REFERENCE	QUANTITY	PART	STOCK	THICKNESS	(mm)	WIDTH	(mm)	LENGTH	(mm)	COMMENTS
A	2	front/back	plywood	$^1/_2$	13	$5^1/_2$	140	$6^1/_2$	165	
B	1	lower right side	plywood	$^1/_2$	13	4	102	6	152	
C	1	lower left side	plywood	$^1/_2$	13	$4^1/_2$	114	6	152	
D	2	left/right roof	plywood	$^1/_2$	13	5	127	6	152	
E	1	back	plywood	$^1/_2$	13	$4^3/_4$	121	6	152	
F	1	roof	hdwd dowel	$^1/_4$ d	6			2	51	

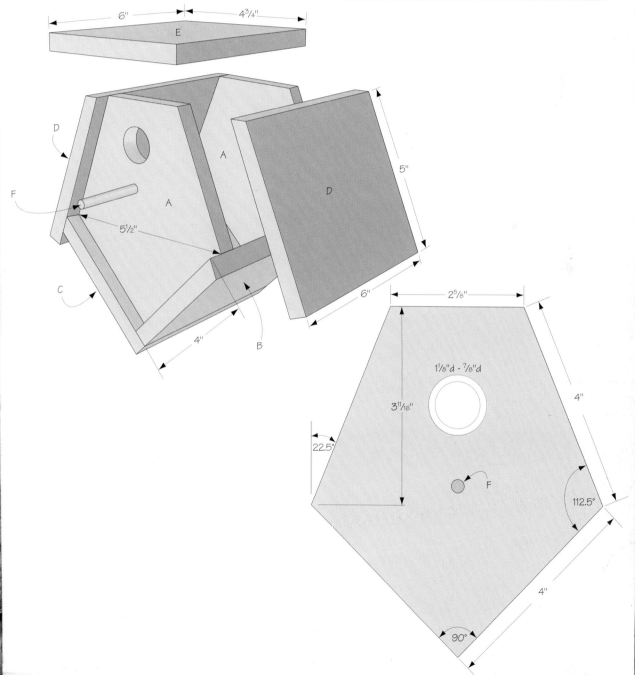

purple martin condo

THIS HOME FOR PURPLE MARTINS IS ONE OF the easiest and fastest projects in this book. And, because if its modular nature, it's also one of the most unique. Purple martins are social nesters, and while individual birds prefer to have their "own room," so to speak, they enjoy living in colonies with other purple martins. Further, of all the cavity-nesting birds discussed throughout this book, purple martins rely the most on man-made housing; in fact, they prefer it to natural cavities, which often do not lend themselves to large colonies. With this house's design, you can not only make your purple martin colony as large as you'd like, your options for its final appearance are limitless based on how you arrange the finished modules.

Each module is based on the purple martin's preferred living space, a cube with minimum interior dimensions of 6" × 6" × 6", and is made entirely of ½" pine. Of course, you could substitute any other solid wood species, or even plywood.

Because you will likely make this house in multiple modules, it's best to cut multiples of each component at the same time to cut down on the number of tool setups. That is, cut all the house backs with one setup, change your saw's setting and cut all the sides, change it again to cut all the fronts, etc. With the exception of the top/bottom components, all the house parts are very similar in size, so label your stacks as in Fig. 1 to keep everything straight.

With waterproof glue and nails, begin the assembly by attaching the house sides to the house back. To this assembly, attach the top and bottom pieces. (Fig. 2.) Drill a 2" entrance hole 2" on-center from the bottom of the house front/door, then center the door in the front opening of the house and drive galvanized hinge nails on each side about an inch from the top. Notice that I've sized the front/door a bit smaller than the back, allowing for a narrow gap at both top and bottom when

it's centered in the front opening. The bottom gap will allow for drainage, while both top and bottom gaps provide additional ventilation and allow the door to be easily lifted without rubbing at the top and bottom of the house. In Fig. 3 I'm using a nail set to put the heads of the hinge nails slightly below the surface. Finally, drill a pilot hole through one side and into the door near the bottom of the house, and drive in a 1" exterior screw to keep the door shut. Countersink the screw so it is flush with the house side.

Taking the number of modules you've made into consideration, you can arrange them any way you'd like. (If you know what arrangement you'll use beforehand, place the door screw on the side of the house that will be most accessible in your arrangement.) The modules can be attached directly to each other with nails or screws, or can be individually attached to a plywood platform for low arrangements, or to a backer board for tall ones.

Your purple martin condo should be mounted on a pole 8' to 20' above the ground, and at least 35' to 40' from your house. Ideally, your home will be adjacent to a large field where purple martins will swoop through the air over large open areas to catch insects. This is important — their entire diet is caught this way — so if your home is surrounded by a lot of trees, it's really not the best location for a purple martin house.

Purple martins are the largest species of swallow in North America, and are common throughout the eastern, central, and portions of the Southwestern United States, as well as throughout Mexico and Central America. Deep black with a shimmering blue/purple sheen to the feathers, they're the only swallows without a light-colored underside. They feed entirely on insects, and so are migratory. Although they winter in South America, they will often return to the same northern nesting grounds they used the previous year.

FIGURE 1 With the exception of the top/bottom components, which are identical, all the house parts are very similar in size, so label your stacks to keep everything straight.

FIGURE 2 With waterproof glue and nails, begin the assembly by attaching the house sides to the house back. To this assembly, attach the top and bottom pieces.

FIGURE 3 Use a nail set to put the heads of the hinge nails slightly below the surface.

PURPLE MARTIN CONDO • inches (millimeters)

REFERENCE	QUANTITY	PART	STOCK	THICKNESS	(mm)	WIDTH	(mm)	LENGTH	(mm)	COMMENTS
A	1	back	pine	$1/2$	13	6	152	6	152	
B	1	front/door	pine	$1/2$	13	6	152	$5^7/8$	149	
C	2	sides	pine	$1/2$	13	6	152	7	178	
D	2	top/bottom	pine	$1/2$	13	7	178	$8^1/2$	216	

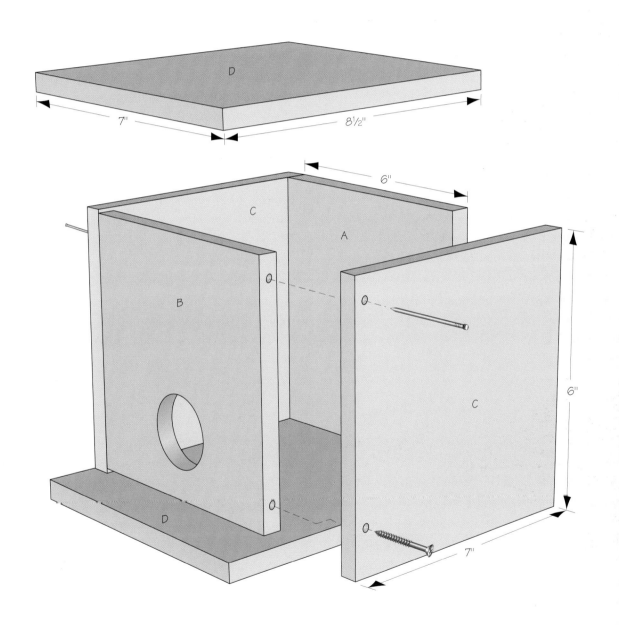

bat house

BATS AREN'T BIRDS, OF COURSE, BUT IN SPITE of the fact that they're among the most beneficial animals you can attract to your yard, they still get a bum rap. Sure, they aren't cuddly or attractive (up close, in fact, you won't find anything uglier), but they earn their keep in two important ways.

First, they put a huge big dent in local insect populations, especially mosquitoes. A single bat can, depending on size and species habit, eat several hundred insects an hour. The common little brown bat regularly downs as many as 20 insects per minute – that's a whopping 1,200 bugs an hour. The second benefit is derived from the first. Because lots of insects hang around flowering plants and trees, bats are also great pollinators. Birds perform both of those jobs, but the majority of insect-eating birds are strictly day-timers, meaning that bats take up the same job on the night shift for round-the-clock benefits.

This project is made entirely of ¾" cedar. A major difference between this house and the others in this book is that this one has a central divider separating the house into two sleep chambers. Also, in other house projects I've recommended orienting the rough face inward on the front to give a climbing surface to nestlings, but since bats don't just sleep at the bottom – they'll be climbing every interior surface of this house looking for a place to hang while they snooze – you should orient all the components with the rough side facing in.

Bats don't need much room. I've designed this house for the little brown bat, the most common bat throughout the U.S. and Canada, so the sleeping chambers are a mere ¾". You can easily adjust dimensions for other bat species.

The best way to construct this house is front-to-back. Cut the house components to size. Like many of the houses in this book, the top is sloped at 10° to allow for better rain runoff, so the top of each side is cut at that angle, while the top edges of the house front and back are beveled at 10°. These cuts can be made with a miter saw, handsaw, or a table saw with a miter gauge.

Use a pencil to mark the inside surfaces of the sides for placement of the divider and house front, as in Fig. 1. I find marking in this way helps me keep parts straight, and facilitates locating them correctly when gluing and nailing. Since all the components are of the same thickness as the sleeping chambers, you can use an extra piece of scrap ¾" stock to do your marking.

All the inner surfaces should be the rough faces of the cedar. Before construction, you'll need to roughen up the smooth face of the divider. The easiest way to do this is to clamp the divider to a work surface and score it repeatedly with a utility knife. Note in Fig. 2 that I'm keeping my free hand behind that clamp at one end for safety.

Begin construction by attaching the front to the inside edge of one of the sides with glue and nails, followed by the center divider. Keeping the divider in place on your marks while you nail can be difficult, so instead install the divider with glue and clamps only as in Fig. 3. (We'll throw a couple reinforcing nails in there later.) The divider should be placed 2¾" from the bottom edge of the side workpiece; once the floor and roof are in place, this will create a 2" gap at both top and bottom of the sleeping chambers for the bats to maneuver inside the house.

When dry, remove the clamps and set the house on its completed side. Run beads of glue on the edges of the house front and divider, position the remaining side, and nail in place. (Fig. 4) At this point, you can place a couple nails through the sides and into the divider on the other side for a bit of added strength.

Hold the floor in place at the bottom of the house without glue, drill a single countersunk pilot hole on each side and secure the floor in place with screws as in Fig. 5. This will allow you to remove the floor for cleaning, which you will need to do periodically. While nesting birds frequently remove droppings from their houses, bats don't.

Attach the slanted roof with glue and nails, then mount the entire house on the back board, driving nails from the rear of the house. Finally, drill a ¼" to ⅜" ventilation hole near the top on each side.

Mount your bat house high on the side of a building, under the eaves if possible where it'll be out of the weather. Or, you can attach it to a tall pole; wooden telephone or utility lighting poles are excellent choices. Bats like a warm place to sleep, so orient the house facing east; this way, the house will warm quickly when the bats head home at dawn.

The main variation you can make with this house is size. Remember that bats will easily fill an entire cave, so there's really no upper limit. Just keep in mind that larger houses require very sturdy mounting, and will need more frequent cleaning. For larger bats, increase the size of the sleeping chamber and the house's bottom entrance. For the little brown bat, an entrance of ⅞" to 1" works well; larger bats need larger entrances. Also, no matter how large the house is, remember to build it so the back extends at least 6" below the house's bottom entrance, providing a landing area for bats to grasp before climbing up inside for the night... er, I mean day.

FIGURE 1 On the sides, lay out the location of the central divider and front and back.

FIGURE 2 When you're scoring the divider, keep your free hand clear of the blade.

FIGURE 3 It's a little easier to install the divider using just glue and some clamps. A couple of reinforcing nails can be added later.

FIGURE 4 Glue and nail the sides in place.

FIGURE 5 Secure the bottom in place with two screws only. You'll need to remove the bottom from time to time for cleaning.

BAT HOUSE • inches (millimeters)

REFERENCE	QUANTITY	PART	STOCK	THICKNESS	(mm)	WIDTH	(mm)	LENGTH	(mm)	COMMENTS
A	2	sides	cedar	³/₄	19	3¹/₂	89	23¹/₂	597	
B	1	front	cedar	³/₄	19	7¹/₂	190	23	584	
C	1	divider	cedar	³/₄	19	7¹/₂	190	19¹/₂	495	
D	1	floor	cedar	³/₄	19	1³/₄	45	7¹/₂	190	
E	1	back	cedar	³/₄	19	9	229	30	762	
F	1	roof	cedar	³/₄	19	6	152	12	305	

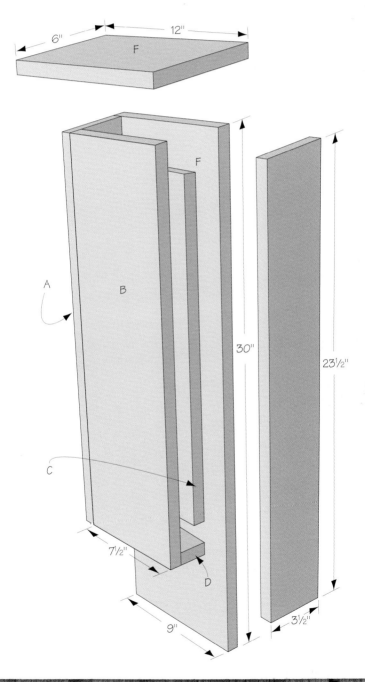

butterfly house

LIKE THE BATS DISCUSSED IN THE PREVIOUS chapter, butterflies are natural pollinators. Unlike the flying mammals, however, butterflies are beautiful and brighten any yard or garden they frequent. Attracting butterflies to your home by planting flowers they like is the first step in enticing them to take up residence. The other half is giving them a place to stay.

Some butterfly species – monarchs, mourning cloaks, longwings and tortoiseshells, for example – can live from several months to a full year. As a result, they address cold weather a couple different ways. Some migrate to warmer climates, finding shelter at night while they travel; others stay where they are and hibernate. But most butterflies, whether traveling or staying put, look for shelter during colder seasons, and even on chillier summer and fall nights. In the wild they'll look for crevices in trees or rocks. You can provide them shelter with a butterfly house – and at the same time add an attractive touch to your garden.

Butterfly houses can be almost any size, although about 3" square and 12" tall would be a good minimum. I've used ½" pine for the house here, but any untreated wood up to ¾" is fine. I like the look of unfinished wood, especially after it begins to weather, so I've left this one natural, but painted houses provide an additional splash of color to your landscaping. (Some butterfly aficionados insist that painting flowers on the houses attracts more butterflies, but the claim is difficult to quantify.)

Once again, I've used a 10° angle for the roof slope, but instead of cutting angles and bevels first, this house is small enough to do that slope another, easier way later in the construction process. For that reason, note that the vertical components are all the same length.

The most complicated part of this house is the front with its multiple ½" × 3¼" entrance slots. Mark the front for slot locations, starting with the middle one centered left-to-right, and 5¼" from the bottom. All four of the outer entrances are set in 1½" from the side edges. The two lower entrances are 1" from the bottom edge, while the two upper ones are 2" from the top edge. (Once the roof is sloped, all holes will be evenly centered on the house front.)

Start the entrance slots by drilling a ½" hole at each end, then clamp the workpiece to a secure surface and use a jigsaw to connect the holes, as in Fig. 1. Sand all the entrance edges smooth.

Butterflies like a natural, rough surface to cling to, and there are a couple ways you can do this. A large strip of solid bark the size of the sides can be glued or stapled in place like wallpaper on one or both sides of the house. I opted for halving some branches on the band saw, and stapling them in place as shown in Fig. 2. Since we'll be cutting the roof slope later, be sure the highest staple is placed at least 1½" from the top.

Attach the front of the house to the two sides with glue and nails, then attach the back the same way. Again, upper nails should be at least 1½" from the top edge to avoid cutting through them in the next step. Mark a cutline for the roof slope, and cut the 10° angle on your marks with a band saw or other saw, as in Fig. 3, and sand as necessary. You can make the roof angle steeper or shallower if you like. For that matter, you can eliminate the angle and go with a flat roof if you prefer.

Attach the roof with glue and nails. Make the bottom removable for cleaning by mounting it to the house with four screws, one through each side as in Fig. 4. When it comes to keeping a clean home, butterflies could win the Good Housekeeping award. However, leaves and other debris can get into the house through the multiple entrances, plus bark can deteriorate over time and you may wish to replace it.

Locate your finished butterfly house near your flowers, as a ready source of nectar will attract the butterflies to the area. The house should be mounted on a slender post driven into the ground, but should be no more than a foot or two off the ground. Again, the key is to keep the house as close to the flowers as possible.

FIGURE 1 Drill two ½"-diameter holes spaced 2¾" on center. Connect the holes with lines and make the cuts.

FIGURE 2 Bark or branches covered in bark make great perches for the butterflies.

FIGURE 3 Assemble the entire box, then cut the 10° top slope on the whole thing at one time using your band saw.

FIGURE 4 Attach the roof with four screws.

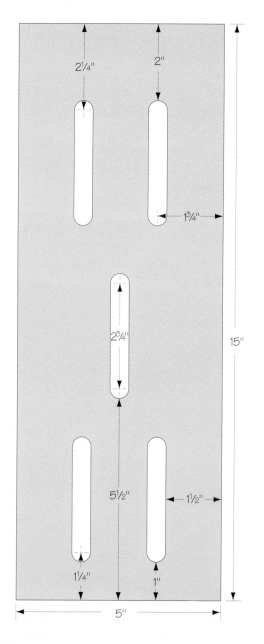

2¼"   2"

1¾"

2¾"

15"

5½"   1½"

1¼"   1"

5"

BUTTERFLY HOUSE • inches (millimeters)

REFERENCE	QUANTITY	PART	STOCK	THICKNESS	(mm)	WIDTH	(mm)	LENGTH	(mm)	COMMENTS
A	1	front	pine	$1/2$	13	$5^1/2$	140	15	381	
B	2	sides	pine	$1/2$	13	$3^1/2$	89	15	381	
C	1	back	pine	$1/2$	13	$5^1/2$	140	15	381	
D	1	roof	pine	$1/2$	13	$5^1/2$	140	7	178	
E	1	floor	pine	$1/2$	13	5	127	$6^1/4$	159	
F	n/a	roost	bark/branch							cut to fit; any natural material with bark is fine

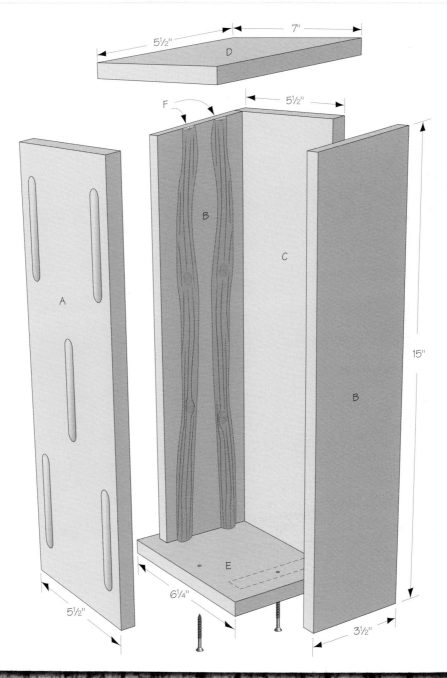

nesting shelf

NOT ALL BIRDS ARE CAVITY NESTERS, ENJOYING the quiet and security of an enclosed space — a birdhouse — to call home. Some prefer to be out in the open and build their nests on ledges, fissures in rocks, between boards in barns or in the crooks of branches. The list of these open-nesting birds is long, but among the most common and wide-ranging are the robin, cardinal, eastern phoebe, blue jay, mourning dove and barn swallow.

Nest shelves are very simple, and can be nothing more than a bare shelf. Even a roof isn't necessary, as many birds in this category will build open nests in trees sheltered only by whatever leaves happen to be above them. However, they welcome man-made nest shelves with a protective roof. They still don't care to be completely enclosed on the sides, so nest-shelf sides should be cut in such a way as to give them a wide-angled view of their surroundings.

The nest shelf presented here in ¾" cedar, with its 6½" × 7" shelf will work for just about any species preferring an open nest; consider adjusting the size slightly depending on the species you're building for. This one is sized fine for barn swallows, eastern phoebes and smaller birds. For robins, doves, cardinals and jays, increase the size of the shelf an inch or so in width and length; height can remain the same. (In truth, open nesters aren't that fussy; a nest shelf like the one in this project will appeal to about all of them.)

Begin by cutting the nest shelf components to size. Transfer the pattern of the nest shelf sides onto your workpieces and cut out the pattern with a jigsaw or on the band saw, as shown in Fig. 1. As with other projects in this book, I've stuck with a 10° angle at the tops of the sides for the roof slope, but feel free to adjust this as you wish.

Attach the sides to the main shelf with glue and nails. Bevel the top edge of the back to accommodate the roof slope, then glue and nail it to the main shelf/side assembly. Note in Fig. 2 that I'm using clamps to keep the back aligned until I can get it nailed into place.

Flip the assembly on its back and attach the shelf front. (Fig. 3) Complete the nest shelf assembly by attaching the top with glue and nails. In Fig. 4, you can see a trick I often use when using a nailer. I've set my table saw fence so the assembly is near the edge of the saw's extension table and then locked it in place. This gives a solid support behind the assembly to keep it in place while I work.

With the nest shelf complete, drill some drainage holes in the main shelf, as well as mounting holes through the back; one through the back inside the house, and another in the extension below the main shelf will do it.

Robins and mourning doves can be quite sociable with people, so don't hesitate to mount the nest shelf on the side of your house near a window. If you keep quick movements to a minimum, you can watch the mother and nestlings from inside the window as the brood grows. Barn swallows prefer their nests higher, under the eaves of a house or other structure whenever possible. Jays and cardinals prefer more open spaces, so a tree is best for mounting. However, as with the nest-shelf size, open nesters aren't fussy with shelf location.

FIGURE 1 Transfer the pattern to the side pieces and use a band saw or jigsaw the cut the sides to shape.

FIGURE 2 Attach the sides to the shelf. Then use clamps to hold the back to the sides/shelf assembly and nail it in place.

FIGURE 3 Lay the shelf assembly on its back and attach the shelf front.

FIGURE 4 I use my table saw's fence to hold the shelf steady as I nail the roof in place.

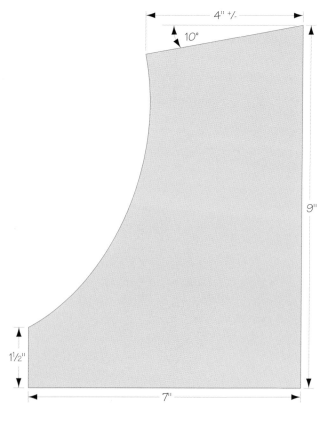

NESTING SHELF • inches (millimeters)

REFERENCE	QUANTITY	PART	STOCK	THICKNESS	(mm)	WIDTH	(mm)	LENGTH	(mm)	COMMENTS
A	1	back	cedar	³/₄	19	8	203	10¹/₂	267	
B	2	sides	cedar	³/₄	19	7	178	9	229	
C	1	shelf	cedar	³/₄	19	6¹/₂	165	7	178	
D	1	shelf front	cedar	³/₄	19	1¹/₂	38	8	203	
E	1	roof	cedar	³/₄	19	7	178	10	254	

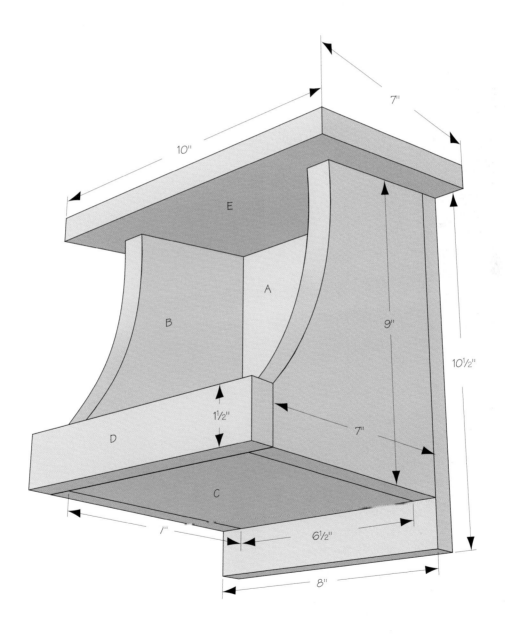

chickadee house

CHICKADEES ARE AMONG THE MOST ENTERTAIN-ing of backyard birds. Acrobatic and highly agile, the seemingly defy gravity as they hop and scamper along branches, deck railings and feeders. Because they're year-round residents, they appreciate a birdhouse in summer months, and a well-stocked feeder in winter. A suet feeder like the one in the next section is almost guaranteed to draw them from miles around in cold weather. Chickadees grow accustomed to humans quickly, and if you have enough patience they'll even eat seeds out of your hand.

I've seen wedge-shaped chickadee houses before, and adapted that idea into this design similar to an inverted Peterson bluebird box. The steeply sloping roof adds a striking touch to any backyard landscaping. With the rough faces oriented inward on each side, ³⁄₄" cedar is a good choice for this project as nestlings can easily climb the rough surface.

Cut the components to size, and drill a 1¹⁄₈" entry hole 3" from the top in one of the sides. The two sides are identical and the hole can go in either one, but take your potential mounting site into consideration before drilling — you'll want the entry hole to face your home

Image copyright Gerald A DeBoer, 2009. Used under license from Shutterstock.com.

so you can watch the antics of the ten-ants. Bevel the top edge of the roof and the bottom edge of the lower front/door at 57.5°.

Using the lower front/door as a spacer, center and position the sides on the house back. Run a bead of glue along the rear edges of the sides, and drive a nail through each end as in Fig. 1. Set the door aside and flip the house over, then add a few more nails from the back side. Note in Fig. 2 that I've used pencil to outline where the sides make contact on the other side, which helps to center the nails.

Now attach the small top with glue and nails and lay the house on its back. As we've already done with other houses, hold the lower front/door in place and drill pilot holes through the sides and into the door about 5" from the bottom of the door, then drive a galvanized nail through each side to act as hinges, as shown in Fig. 3. Drill one more hole through the side near the bot-tom of the door and slip in a galvanized nail to keep the door closed. Just slip out the nail and swing the door down for cleaning.

Attach the roof with glue and nails. In Fig. 4 you can see how the beveled top of the roof fits right into the joint created by the top and sides. Finally, drill ³⁄₈" ven-tilation holes at the top on each side of the house, plus a single mounting hole through the top and bottom of the house back. Because the lower front/door is not sol-idly attached and because it meets the back of the house at a steep angle, no additional drainage holes are neces-sary in this design.

Mount your chickadee house from 5' to 15' off the ground on the side of a tree in an area that receives both sunshine and shade.

Don't be surprised if other birds take a liking to your chickadee house. Nuthatches like a similar nesting site, and house wrens will live anywhere. The 1¹⁄₈" entry hole is perfectly sized for both of these other birds.

FIGURE 1 Apply glue along the rear edges of the sides and drive a nail through each end to secure them to the back.

FIGURE 2 Use a pencil to outline where the sides make contact on the other side to use as a guide for nailing.

FIGURE 3 Install a galvanized nail through each side to act as hinges.

FIGURE 4 The beveled top of the roof fits into the joint created by the top and sides.

a note about chickadees

The two most numerous chickadee species in North America are the black-capped chickadee found primarily throughout the northern U.S. and Canada, and the Carolina chickadee native to the southeast U.S. Both birds have a distinctive black cap and bib separated by white cheeks, and gray back and wings. Their bodies have an orange cast, but brighter on the black-cap and with more gray on the Carolina. Chickadees eat mainly insects during warm weather, supplementing their diet with seeds and berries in winter. The two species, which are so similar that they occasionally interbreed where their ranges overlap, don't migrate.

CHICKADEE HOUSE • inches (millimeters)

REFERENCE	QUANTITY	PART	STOCK	THICKNESS	(mm)	WIDTH	(mm)	LENGTH	(mm)	COMMENTS
A	1	back	cedar	³/₄	19	7	178	16	406	
B	2	sides	cedar	³/₄	19	7	178	11¹/₂	292	
C	1	lower front/door	cedar	³/₄	19	4	102	7	178	
D	1	roof	cedar	³/₄	19	7	178	10¹/₂	257	
E	1	top	cedar	³/₄	19	3	76	7	178	

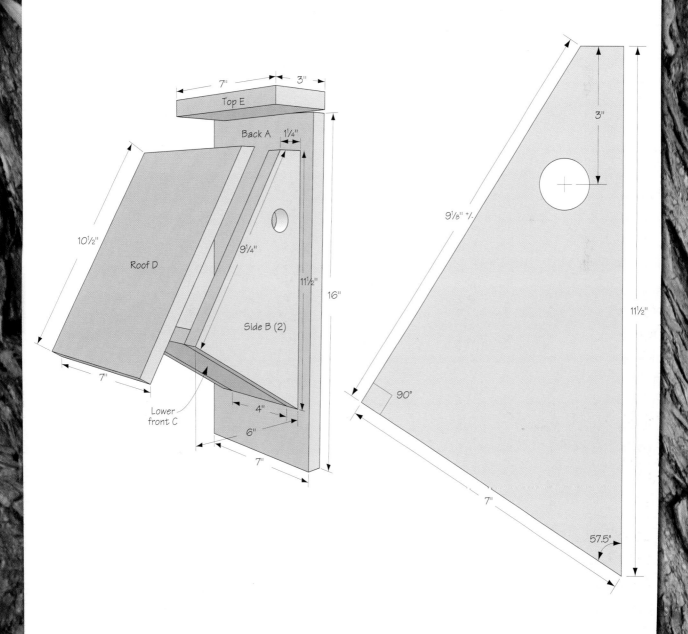

3
FEEDING TIME

Feeding birds serves several purposes, the most obvious of which is to attract these lovely creatures to your backyard. Feeders can also attract birds that might otherwise not have discovered the available housing you've created for them. Many birds prefer nesting near a ready source of food, meaning that the feeders and houses work together to create a suitable home for a number of species.

Feeding is even more essential in the winter as regular food sources become scarce, particularly for non-migrating birds whose diet consists of insects not available during the winter months. For these birds, the ready source of protein and fats supplied by a suet feeder is especially welcome.

Bird food today is labeled as to the type of birds that enjoy it, so check packaging before buying. If you notice that certain types of seeds in a particular mixture are being ignored or simply scattered on the ground, consider changing to a different mixture.

Always monitor your feeders carefully, checking frequently to be certain they don't remain empty for long periods of time.

gravity feeder

USING A TRIED-AND-TRUE DESIGN, GRAVITY feeders can hold a large amount of chow. The wide opening at the bottom accommodates a seed mix containing everything from large sunflower seeds down to tiny millet seed. With its clear sides, it's easy to see when it's time to refill. (Of course, all of your birds suddenly disappearing is another good clue the feeder's empty.) The version here features a hinged roof, making refilling a quick task. We'll use ¾" cedar for this project, with ⅛" acrylic for the windows.

Begin by laying out the end pattern on your workpiece, as in Fig. 1. Note that the end pattern has straight sides, with a curved line inside the outer edges. (We'll cut that curve out later, but the straight edges are necessary for first cutting slots to accommodate the windows.) I used the band saw to cut the end patterns, but you can also use a jigsaw or handsaw. Choose the orientation you want for the end pieces and use a pencil to mark the inside faces.

Cut the slots for the windows on the table saw. Set the fence at 1", and raise the blade to cut a ¼"-deep slot in a single pass, as in Fig. 3. Once the slots are cut, there's no need for that straight edge any longer, so layout and cut the waste from the curved edges. A spindle sander works great to smooth the inside curve. (Fig. 4)

Put a bit of glue on each end of the bottom and nail the ends in place. (Fig. 5) Attach the window spacers at the inside corners with glue and a pair of brads. This spacer will set the height of the side windows, creating a gap at the bottom of each to allow seeds to flow into the feeding tray. These spacers can be made of any weather-resistant wood, and I happened to have some ½" × ½" oak scrap, so I used that. With the spacers in place, attach the tray sides with glue and nails, as in Fig. 6.

Cut the windows to size and test-fit them in the slots as in Fig. 7. Note that I've left the protective film in place on the acrylic. When working with acrylic or other plastic sheets, leave this film in place as long as possible to prevent scratching the plastic while you work.

The roof is made in identical halves, joined in the middle with a continuous hinge (sometimes called a piano hinge). I've found that it's easiest to make and hinge the roof before attaching it to the main part of the feeder. Cut the roof halves to size, and cut a 60° bevel along one edge of each half.

The hinge you get will undoubtedly be too long, so you'll need to cut it to length. You can use a hacksaw for this, or a rotary tool with a cutting disk if you have one. It's not necessary, by the way, for the hinge to run the entire length of the roof. In fact, depending on the hinge you get, it may be difficult to cut it to the exact roof length since the hinges are already drilled — the exact roof length may place screw holes too close to the ends, inviting split-out when driving the screws. The hinge I used here is cut about ¼" short of the roof length on each end to center the holes in the hinge.

Center the hinge on one beveled edge to mark for the screw holes. I used an awl to create some small pilot holes as shown in Fig. 8., but you can also drill them. Cedar is very soft and easily takes screws, but pilot holes eliminate the chance of splitting the wood. Butt the other roof half up against the hinge of the first half, and attach it the same way.

Lay the completed roof on top of the main portion of the feeder to check for fit, and mark one side in pencil, as shown in Fig. 9, to help you accurately place the nails. (I've made my pencil lines very dark for photo purposes, but make your marks as light as possible for easier removal.) Put a bit of glue on the top edges of one side of the feeder, and nail the roof in place on that side. Be sure you have the window in place on that side before nailing. Give the feeder a good sanding to remove any pencil marks and to ease any sharp edges.

Simply flip open one side of the roof to fill. The best seed to use for a gravity feeder of this type is a mixed seed, which will attract the greatest variety of birds. Several mixes are available that are designed to attract specific species, so the choice is yours.

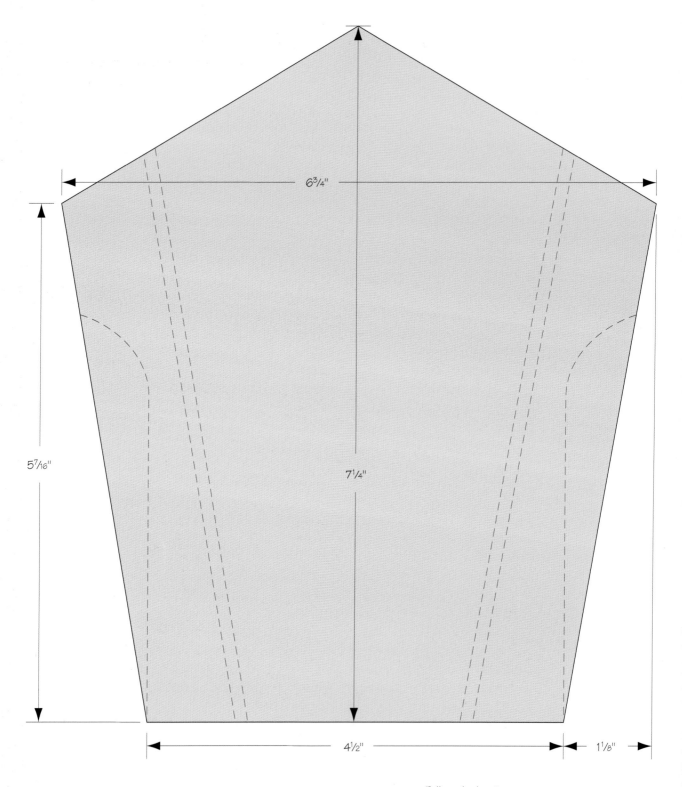

6³/₄"

7¹/₄"

5⁷/₁₆"

4¹/₂"

1¹/₈"

Full-scale drawing

GRAVITY FEEDER • inches (millimeters)

REFERENCE	QUANTITY	PART	STOCK	THICKNESS	(mm)	WIDTH	(mm)	LENGTH	(mm)	COMMENTS
A	2	ends	cedar	$^3/_4$	19	$6^3/_4$	171	$7^1/_4$	184	blank size before cutting to shape
B	1	bottom	cedar	$^3/_4$	19	$4^1/_2$	114	$7^1/_2$	191	
C	2	tray sides	cedar	$^3/_4$	19	$1^1/_2$	38	9	229	
D	2	roof halves	cedar	$^3/_4$	19	5	127	11	279	
E	2	spacers	hardwood	$^1/_2$	13	$^1/_2$	13	$4^1/_2$	114	
F	2	windows	acrylic	$^1/_8$	3	4	102	8	203	
G	1	continuous hinge	brass					$10^1/_2$	267	

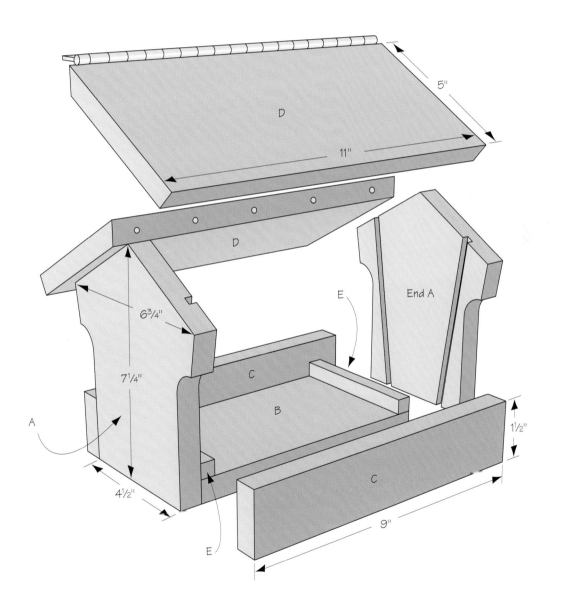

FIGURE 1 Make a full-sized pattern of the end and use it to trace the shape on the workpiece.

FIGURE 2 Use a band saw or jigsaw to cut out the ends.

FIGURE 3 Use the table saw to cut the slots for the acrylic panels.

FIGURE 4 An oscillating spindle sander does a good job sanding the curves.

FIGURE 5 Glue and nail the ends to the bottom.

FIGURE 6 Attach the tray sides with glue and nails.

FIGURE 7 Fit the acrylic to the feeder, *then* remove the covering.

FIGURE 8 Use an awl to mark the screw holes. Cedar is soft enough for you to screw into without drilling, but pilot holes are recommended to prevent splitting the wood.

FIGURE 9 Lightly draw (mine are dark so you can see them in the photo) locating lines on the roof sections, then glue and nail the roof in place.

finch feeder

THERE ARE MANY WAYS TO ATTRACT BIRDS, but the best by far is to simply offer them a free meal. Finches, with their bright coloration and acrobatic antics, are among the most enjoyable to watch, and this tube-style feeder will turn your backyard into the local five-star restaurant.

The main component is a clear plastic tube. Because these vary widely in size and wall thickness, it's best to acquire your tube first before making any of the wooden parts. You can use just about any sturdy plastic tube, including widely available acrylic mailing tubes. Most of the tubes you'll find (except for mailing tubes, which are very thin) have walls measuring $1/16$" or $1/8$" thick. A tube at least 2" in diameter is fine.

For this project, I used a 13"-long tube, 2" in diameter, with $1/16$" walls. *The dimensions that appear for all the wooden components here reflect this, so be sure to adjust the size of your components to match the tube you use.*

The top and bottom of this feeder are lathe-turned hardwood, which is more durable in this usage than softwood. I used ash, which weathers well; however, oak or teak would also be good choices. This is simple spindle turning, among the easiest and most straightforward of lathe work, but to assure that these two components fit properly it's essential to work slowly and carefully. Start by cutting a ring from your tube that will serve as a gauge.

Turn the spindle for the feeder top to a uniform thickness that matches the tube diameter; for my tube, I'm turning the spindle to a cylinder 2" in diameter. Because the top component overhangs the edge of the tube, create a $1/16$" shoulder as indicated in the drawing. Go slowly, periodically use the gauging ring to check the diameter of the portion that will fit inside the tube. When the ring fits, stop turning that insert portion. (It's best if you stop when the ring is very snug — you can always sand it for a better fit later, but if you make it too loose there's no fixing it.) With the insert portion of the top completed, finish the rest of the top profile and sand it smooth.

If your stock is long enough, you can make both the top and bottom components at the same time. My stock was a bit short for both pieces, so in Fig. 3 I'm using a parting tool to form the underside of the top. At this point, remove the workpiece from the lathe and cut the top free with a knife or fine-cut saw.

Turn the feeder bottom the same way. Note that the bottom piece fits entirely inside the tube and does not have an overhanging lip. Again, check the diameter carefully with the gauging ring as you turn and stop when the ring fits the entire length of the bottom piece. Sand it smooth.

The 13" tube used here creates eight feeding positions, but you can use any length you want; just be sure to adjust dimensions and hole locations accordingly.

Getting the holes drilled perfectly straight can be tricky, so I made a simple jig that acts as a drilling cradle for the tube. The jig's easy to make. Attach a narrow wood strip on one side of a long piece of scrap (I used strips measuring $3/4$" × $3/4$") with a couple nails. Place the tube against the first strip and attach a second strip to the scrap on the other side of the tube so it holds the tube in place. Draw a line on the jig exactly in the middle of the two strips for alignment purposes. Draw four lines the length of the tube, 90° apart. A "Sharpie" marker works well for this, and easily wipes clean with mineral spirits later.

Starting about $1/4$" from the bottom, mark for the perch holes on a set of lines on opposite sides of the tube, placing them 6" apart. Rotate the tube 90° and, moving about 3" up from your first set of marks, mark another set of perch holes. This will stagger the perches around the tube.

Now make additional marks for the seed holes about 2" above each perch-hole mark. (It's helpful if you use a different color marker, as in Fig. 4.)

Place the tube in your drilling jig, aligning the line on one side of the tube with the one on the jig, and hold it in place with masking tape. Using a $1/4$" bit, drill

FIGURE 1 I've used some masking tape to hold a ring (cut from the tube) over the tailstock. I can easily see my progress as I'm turning.

FIGURE 2 The other reason for having the ring taped to the tailstock — I can slide it over the part without having to remove the part from the lathe.

FIGURE 3 Separating the top part from the blank. If you have a blank long enough (about 11"), turn both the top and bottom from one piece, then separate them.

FIGURE 4 Using different colored markers helps you know what mark is what.

FIGURE 5 Make a cradle from some scrap wood to hold the plastic tube in place with you drill the perch holes. Taping the tube in the cradle is a safe way to hold it securely.

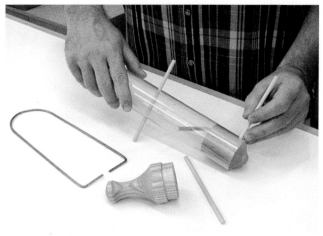

FIGURE 6 Bend the hanger and you're ready to assemble the feeder. The bottom dowel holds the whole thing together.

FINCH FEEDER • inches (millimeters)

REFERENCE	QUANTITY	PART	STOCK	THICKNESS	(mm)	WIDTH	(mm)	LENGTH	(mm)	COMMENTS
A	1	top blank	hardwood	$2^1/2$	64	$2^1/2$	64	6	152	finished dimensions 2d × 4
B	1	bottom blank	hardwood	$2^1/2$	64	$2^1/2$	64	$4^1/2$	114	finished dimensions $1^7/8$ d × $2^1/2$
C	4	perches	dowel	$1/4$ d	6			$5^1/2$	140	hardwood
D	1	tube	plastic	2d	51			13	330	$1/16$"- thick tube walls
E	1	hanger		$1/8$	3			14	356	copper or brass wire

all the perch holes (except the lowest hole) through both sides of the tube simultaneously, as shown in Fig. 5. You'll need to un-tape and re-tape as you rotate the tube. Before drilling the lowest hole, first slip the feeder bottom into place. Making sure that the top of this piece clears the mark you made for the lowest seed hole, drill through both tube and bottom at the same time. Ideally, you want the lowest seed hole to be just above the top of the feeder bottom.

Now drill $1/8$" seed holes on their marks. For easy access to the seed, these holes should be elongated. Do this by drilling a pair of adjacent holes at each mark, one above the other, to form a kind of figure eight. Then, with the drill turning you can "pull" the tube slightly to connect the two holes into a single elongated one. Alternatively, you can use a sharp knife to cut the connector between the two adjacent holes.

Assemble the feeder by slipping the perches into place as in Fig. 6. You'll note how the lowest perch holds the feeder bottom in place.

For a hanger, bend a piece of sturdy wire into a U-shape as shown in Fig. 6. I found that $1/8$" brass rod works well, but copper or other non-rusting metal is fine. *Avoid using a coat hanger, which will surely rust.* Mount the hanger in a pair of holes sized to accommodate the wire you use.

No finish is necessary for the wooden components, but any exterior-grade varnish can be used on the top or bottom if you'd like some gloss and a bit more protection from the elements. Apply the finish to exterior portions of the components only, and not on any portion that slides inside the tube. Do not finish the perches.

The best seed for this type of feeder is thistle seed – also called "nyjer" or "niger." This is a slender black seed that finches love, and it's easy to get at through the tube holes. Thistle seed is a favorite of goldfinches and house finches, but don't be surprised to see a lot of song sparrows enjoying it too!

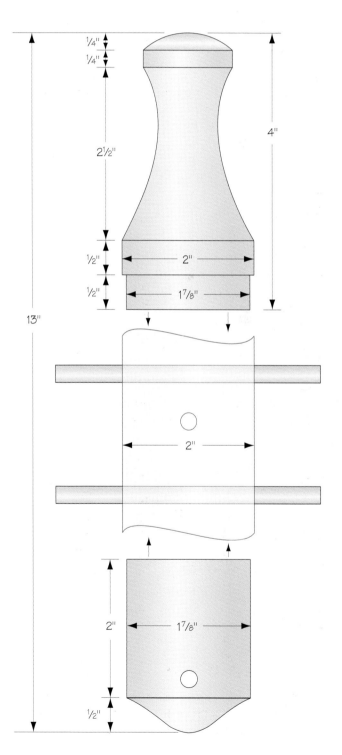

suet feeder

FOR BIRDS THAT PREFER INSECTS AS A MAJOR part of their diet, cold weather can be rough: The lower the thermometer, the fewer bugs to eat. The fat content of bug chow is an important energy source for many birds. Migratory birds head to warmer areas to keep up with the insect supply, but those who stay through the colder months could use a bit of help. A perfect replacement for the insects in their diet is suet.

Suet comes from the hard beef fat found near the kidneys, and when properly cooked down (it melts at a very low temperature) and reconstituted, it forms a solid cake of pure energy for birds with high metabolisms like woodpeckers, chickadees, nuthatches and wrens. Add other items like seeds, nuts or raisins to the suet, and even birds like cardinals and bluebirds will be enticed to join the dinner party. Suet can be fed year-round, but it can be problematic in hot weather — it can melt, drip and turn rancid in direct sun. Summertime suet feeders are best mounted in shaded areas only, and maybe skipped entirely during the hottest months.

Because of its soft but cake-like nature (think a big chunk of hard butter), suet is best offered to birds in a cage-type feeder that holds the suet solidly, but still allows birds to get at it. This suet feeder is similar to the gravity feeder project, in that the food is contained in a grooved housing; instead of two sheets of clear plastic, we'll use two pieces of wire mesh with ½" gaps. The mesh you get may vary slightly in size depending how it's made, so it's best to get your wire first before cutting the wooden components, allowing you to resize the wooden parts as needed.

Using diagonal cutters or snips, cut two pieces that are 10 by 11 of the ½" squares, trimming the pieces as closely as possible on each edge as shown in Fig. 1. The resulting square pieces of wire should come out to be 5" × 5½".

The rest of the feeder is made with ¾" cedar. Cut a piece of cedar 2½" wide and at least 18" long. We'll use this piece to make the feeder bottom and both sides, but let's add the necessary grooves first. It's far easier — and safer — to make these grooves in one long piece than short individual components. Set your table saw's blade at ¼" high, then set the fence ½" from the blade. Run your long workpiece along the fence on each side to create a pair of ¼"-deep grooves as in Fig. 2.

Remove the fence and readjust the blade height to crosscut the two sides to length. Before cutting the bottom piece, verify that your wire-mesh squares are exactly 5" wide. If so, a bottom piece 4½", as noted on the cut list, will hold the sides the correct distance apart to accept the wire. If the mesh is larger than 5", make this bottom piece larger. Taking into account the ¼"-deep grooves, the bottom piece should be ½" less than the wire width. (For example, if your wire square actually measures 5⅛", your bottom piece should be 4⅝".)

With glue and nails, mount the bottom between the two sides — all the grooves should line up perfectly — and check that your mesh squares slide easily into the grooves.

Turn the feeder upside down and center it on the roof, then pencil a mark centered and right up against the sides of the feeder. (Fig. 5) This is where the wire hanger will pass through. Make a similar centered mark about 1½" from the top of each side. Using a bit that matches the thickness of your wire hanger, drill holes on your roof marks, as well as each side of the feeder. (Fig. 6)

Cut out the tail rest. Remember, if you had to alter the length of the bottom piece to accommodate the wire mesh size, make the same alteration to the tail rest. Center a pair of countersunk holes in the bottom of the feeder. (Fig. 7.) Put a bit of glue on the edge of the tail rest, center it on the underside of the feeder as in Fig. 8, and anchor the tail rest in place with screws from the inside of the feeder.

Bend the hanger wire into a curved shape and slip the ends through the holes you drilled into the roof earlier.

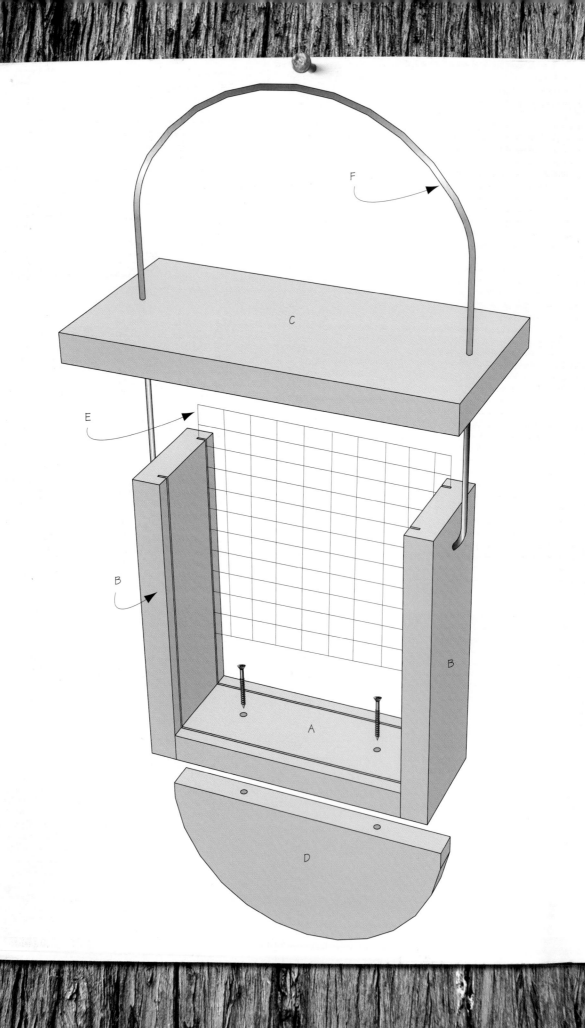

SUET FEEDER • inches (millimeters)

REFERENCE	QUANTITY	PART	STOCK	THICKNESS	(mm)	WIDTH	(mm)	LENGTH	(mm)	COMMENTS
A	1	bottom	cedar	3/4	19	2 1/2	64	4 1/2	114	
B	2	sides	cedar	3/4	19	2 1/2	64	6 1/4	159	
C	1	roof	cedar	3/4	19	4	102	9	229	
D	1	tail rest	cedar	3/4	19	4	102	6	152	
E	1	1/2" wire mesh	galv metal			5	127	5	127	
F	1	wire hanger	metal					28	711	any malleable metal; brass or copper 3/32" or 1/8"

Now bend a 90° angle in each end of the wire and slip the ends into the holes in the feeder sides as in Fig. 9, and slide the roof down. The design of the feeder allows the roof to be slid up to replenish the suet as needed.

For variations, consider making the feeder a different size. I've sized the one here to accommodate the most commonly available suet cakes, usually 4" × 4" squares about 1¼" thick. If you find larger cakes or make your own, feel free to make the feeder any size you like.

Also, I've included the tail rest to make the feeder accessible to the widest variety of birds. Small birds like wrens, chickadees and nuthatches have no need of a tail rest. In fact, they'll access the suet from any angle, including hanging upside down. Larger woodpeckers, however, will hang onto the feeder vertically and will rest their tails on this piece for balance. If you don't have large woodpeckers in your area or only wish to attract smaller birds, you can omit the tail rest.

FIGURE 1 Cut the wire mesh to size using wire cutters.

FIGURE 2 Cut the grooves for the wire mesh.

FIGURE 3 Crosscut the bottom and two side parts to length.

FIGURE 4 Slide the wire mesh in the grooves.

FIGURE 5 Turn the feeder upside down and center it on the roof, then pencil a mark centered and right up against the sides of the feeder.

FIGURE 6 Using a bit that matches the thickness of your wire hanger, drill holes on your roof marks, as well as each side of the feeder.

FIGURE 7 Drill two countersunk holes in the center of the bottom.

FIGURE 8 Glue and screw the tail rest in place. (Screw through the holes you drilled in Step 7.)

FIGURE 9 Feed the wire hanger through the holes in the top. Make 90° bends in the ends and insert them into the holes in the sides.

hummingbird feeder

FASTER THAN A SPEEDING BULLET BARELY describes hummingbirds, among the tiniest birds you can attract to a feeder. How tiny? The typical ruby-throated hummingbird, one of the most common, weighs in at about 3 grams, or about $\frac{1}{10}$ of an ounce. They can zip in and out of a feeder at lighting speed with their wings all but invisible, and no wonder — the typical ruby-throat beats its wings about 50 times per second (3,000 times a minute!). This wing speed and agility make the hummingbird the only bird that can fly backward.

Hummingbirds subsist almost entirely on nectar, and many prefer the nectar of red, orange or pink flowers. For feeders, sugar water — often colored red — is their favorite. This feeder, made of $\frac{3}{4}$" cedar, features twin tubes of liquid so more than one bird can feed at a time. (If the first one at the feeder allows it, that is; the first one there often chases newcomers away.)

You can use almost any kind of tube, but 1"-diameter test tubes or watering tubes (of the kind used for household birds and other pets, which I've used here) are the easiest to find. Almost any bird supplier carries rubber stoppers and angled feeding tubes that fit a 1" test tube. Look for feeding tubes that include a small cap on the end, pierced with a tiny hole in the center.

Begin by cutting feeder components to size and shape. Because the top and bottom are identical, it's easiest to cut and drill them simultaneously. Join a pair of slightly oversized workpieces together by driving small nails into the corners, and then transfer the top/bottom pattern to the top workpiece. When drilling, you want to drill all the way through the top piece but only halfway through the bottom, so set your drill press depth stop so it only goes about $\frac{3}{8}$" into the bottom piece. (Fig. 1) Now move to the band saw and cut out the two pieces as in Fig. 2. With the top and bottom cut out and separated, sand both oval workpieces as needed to smooth the shapes. In the bottom

piece, drill a $\frac{7}{16}$" hole in the center of each of the larger holes. This hole-within-a-hole will support the bottoms of the test tubes, but allow the smaller feeding tube to go through the bottom of the feeder. You can see this piece in the foreground of Fig. 3.

Attach the $1\frac{1}{2}$" sides to the center workpiece as in Fig. 3, resulting in an H-shaped assembly. Center the feeder bottom — large holes facing the center assembly — and glue and nail in place as in Fig. 4.

With the feeder still inverted, center the feeder on the top piece and pencil a mark centered and up against the sides of the center assembly exactly as with the suet feeder in the previous chapter. This is where the wire hanger will pass through. Make a similar centered mark about 1" from the top of each side. Using a bit that matches the thickness of your wire hanger, drill holes on the marks in the feeder top and on each side of the feeder.

Just as with the hanger on the suet feeder, bend the hanger wire into a curved shape and slip the ends through the holes you drilled into the top, and make a 90° bend in the tip of each wire oriented inward. Slip the angled ends into the holes in the feeder sides.

Thread the narrow angled feeder tubes through the holes in the bottom then, holding the tubes in place with one hand, slide the top down over both tubes so they fit through the holes in the top, as in Fig. 5.

Since hummingbirds migrate during the winter you'll probably want to bring the feeder in for cleaning and storage, but here's another use for it. Store the stoppers and their angled feeder tubes where you'll find them easily when spring returns. Now reverse the two test tubes open-end up. Fill the tubes with water and your hummingbird feeder serves nicely as a small flower vase.

FIGURE 1 Drill all the way through the top piece but only halfway through the bottom.

FIGURE 2 Now cut the top and bottom pieces to shape using the band saw.

FIGURE 3 With glue and nails, attach the 1½" sides to the center piece.

FIGURE 4 Center the feeder bottom and glue and nail it in place.

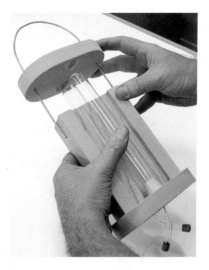

FIGURE 5 Thread the narrow angled feeder tubes through the holes in the bottom. Then, holding the tubes in place with one hand, slide the top down over both tubes so they fit through the holes in the top.

FIGURE 6 Since hummingbirds migrate during the winter you'll probably want to bring the feeder in for cleaning and storage, but here's another use for it — fill the tubes with water and your hummingbird feeder serves nicely as a small flower vase.

HUMMINGBIRD FEEDER • inches (millimeters)

REFERENCE	QUANTITY	PART	STOCK	THICKNESS	(mm)	WIDTH	(mm)	LENGTH	(mm)	COMMENTS
A	1	top	cedar	3/4	19	3 1/2	89	5 1/4	133	
B	1	bottom	cedar	3/4	19	3 1/2	89	5 1/4	133	
C	1	center	cedar	3/4	19	2 1/2	64	6	152	
D	2	center sides	cedar	3/4	19	1 1/2	38	6	152	
E	1	wire hanger; copper or brass	metal	1/8	3 d			18	457	

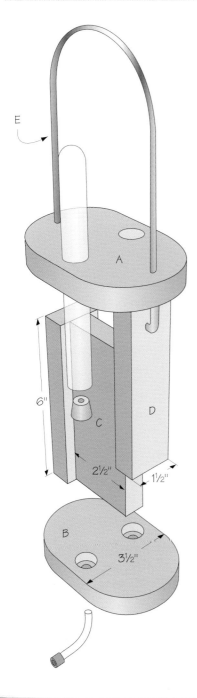

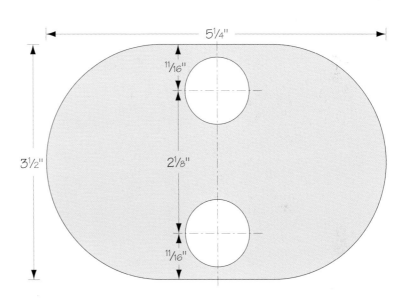

a note about hummingbirds

Hummingbirds are found throughout the Western Hemisphere (although tropical Central and South America have far more species). Two of the most common species in North America are the ruby-throated, found mostly in the eastern U.S., and the very similar black-chinned, found mostly in the west. They build tiny cuplike nests in trees (sometimes using spider silk as one of the materials), and lay only two or three eggs per brood. Because they feed exclusively on flower nectar, both species migrate to warmer climates in the winter.

squirrel feeder

WHEN IT COMES TO RAIDING BIRD FEEDERS, squirrels are relentless. Without some sort of guard in place, they'll hit the feeder faster than the birds do every time you fill it. Some squirrels can even manage to get around guards and deterrents with an agility that would make Spider-Man jealous. Taking a lesson from the if-you-can't-beat-them school of thought, sometimes the best way to keep these ravenous robbers out of your feeders is to give them one of their own.

This corncob feeder provides a good distraction for those furry thieves when placed away from your other feeders. In fact, with the squirrels thus occupied they become an enjoyable backyard entertainment in their own right. Who knows? You might actually start liking them again.

Made of ¾" cedar components, all of which are small and straight, this is one of the easiest projects in this book. As such, it's a perfect project to make after making several others, since you might be able to make it entirely with scraps. You can make this project even simpler by eliminating the tray front and sides, but I've found that squirrels — like birds — can be sloppy eaters, and the tray sides help to keep stray corn kernels contained in the feeder until eaten, and not scattered over your lawn and landscaping.

I haven't used a lot of screws in these projects, but combined with a bead of glue on the back edge of the tray, their superior strength over nails makes them a natural to attach the tray to the feeder back as in Fig. 1.

Carefully center the tray front on the front edge of the tray and attach with glue and nails. Then, do the same with each of the two tray sides. (Fig. 2.)

Drill a hole about 1½" from the front of the tray bottom to accept a 3" lag screw, which will hold the corncob. Because the last portion of the screw is un-threaded, you'll need a way to keep the screw secured; the best way to do this is with a bit of epoxy. Mix a small amount according to package directions, and, with the screw protruding about 1" or so from the underside of the feeder tray, apply a bit of epoxy to the protruding shaft and the screw head, as shown in Fig. 3. Now just push the screw the rest of the way into the hole until the head is snug against the underside of the feeder. You may need to twist it in or tap it into place with a hammer. Finally, drill countersunk holes in the top and bottom of the feeder back to allow the feeder to be screwed in to a tree.

Most commercial squirrel feeders use a thin rod to hold the corncob, but they don't work well — squirrels can easily dislodge the cob and send it flying to the ground. The lag screw I chose here holds the corncob securely by just twisting it into place. (Fig. 4)

Mount the feeder on a tree away from your regular feeders, but not too far. The idea is that when Mr. Squirrel sees both your guarded feeder and this tempting unguarded one at the same time, he'll go for the easy pickings.

FIGURE 1 Use glue and screws to attach the tray to the back.

FIGURE 2 Attach the front and sides to the tray using nails. These parts help keep the stray kernels of corn under control.

FIGURE 3 Epoxy the lag bolt in place.

FIGURE 4 Simply attach the corn to the bolt by twisting it in place. This will hold it securely while the squirrels eat the corn kernels.

SQUIRREL FEEDER • inches (millimeters)

REFERENCE	QUANTITY	PART	STOCK	THICKNESS	(mm)	WIDTH	(mm)	LENGTH	(mm)	COMMENTS
A	1	back	cedar	$3/4$	19	5	127	10	254	
B	1	tray	cedar	$3/4$	19	$5^1/_2$	140	5	127	
C	1	tray front	cedar	$3/4$	19	$1^1/_2$	38	52	1320	
D	2	tray sides	cedar	$3/4$	19	$1^1/_2$	38	8	203	
E	1	lag screw	galvanized					3	75	

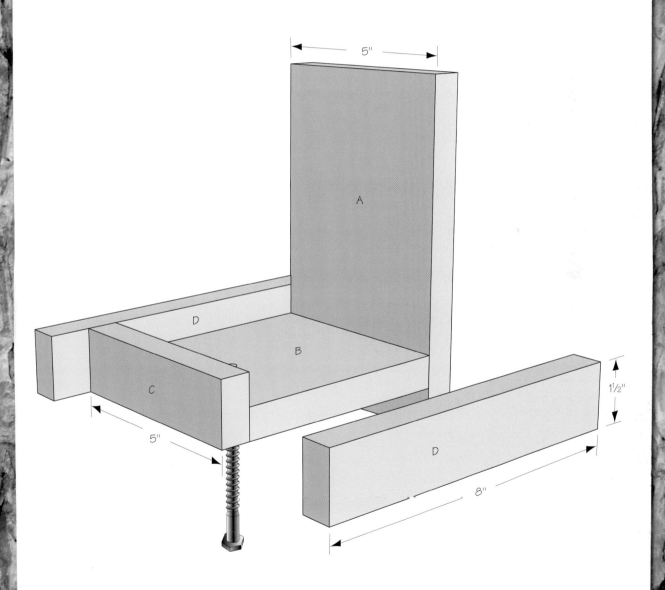

4
FEATHERED FUN

While most of the projects in this book are designed to blend in with their natural surroundings, sometimes the goal is to decorate the yard. The houses presented here run a wide range of playful designs, many of which can add a splash of color outdoors

All of these houses involve at least some amount of painting, so be sure to use exterior-grade paints. By nature of their design, some — like the camera birdhouse — are darker-colored and are best placed in areas that are not in full sunshine all day long.

Because wrens are probably the least fussy of all birds when it comes to houses they choose to live in, I've designed most of these to accommodate them. However, feel free to scale them a bit larger and alter the entrance hole sizes and placement for the birds of your choice. Of course, birdhouses like these are often made for decorative displays with no real intention of having birds live in them. If that's the case for you, you can alter their designs and sizes any way that pleases your individual tastes.

helmet house

BENDING PLYWOOD MAY LOOK DIFFICULT AT first, but it's really quite straightforward. Although it's possible to bend $\frac{3}{32}$" and even $\frac{1}{8}$" plywood for larger forms, for projects the size of most birdhouses I recommend nothing thicker than $\frac{1}{16}$" plywood.

$\frac{1}{16}$" plywood is usually made of only three plies; the grain of the two outer layers runs the same direction, while the inner ply runs at a 90° angle to the other two. Plywood bends most easily when the majority of the grain is oriented perpendicular to the direction of the curve. So, when you cut the plywood for this project, cut it so the surface grain runs side-to-side across the width of the workpiece, and not along the length.

When working with bendable plywood, it's important to allow glue to dry thoroughly between steps. Plywood has a natural tendency to spring back, especially if glue isn't completely dry, so you can't rush the process.

You should also prepare the plywood for bending in advance. Although the finished size of the plywood will be 6" × 16½" once trimmed and sanded on the completed birdhouse, cut the workpiece a bit oversized — ¼" on each side and ½" to 1" on each end is good. Now roll the plywood strip up and clamp it as in Fig. 1, and leave it this way for as long as you can before using it. This will help the plywood acclimatize to the curved shape, making the final bending easier.

Attach the two side workpieces together with a single screw and cut the house sides to shape according to the provided pattern. (If you know how you plan to decorate the helmet sides later, you can locate the screw where decoration will go, thus hiding the hole). With the sides still together, sand the edges smooth; a disc sander is perfect for the convex edges, while the oscillating spindle sander in Fig. 2 is perfect for the concave curves.

Separate the house sides and draw layout lines for the inner components (the house front and back) on the inside face. When the inner components are in place as in Fig. 3, you'll note that there will be small gaps at the top — a very tiny gap on the back, and about

¼" at the front — that will provide ventilation. With one side attached, apply glue to the other sides of the inner components and put the remaining house side in place as in Fig. 4. Before the glue sets use a square or triangle to ensure that both sides are perfectly even all the way around. When you're satisfied everything is straight, nail the side in place.

Unclamp your plywood, and you'll notice that it now has a tendency to curl up on its own. Starting at either end of the house, put glue on only the last inch or two of the house sides. Allowing a bit of overhang all around, clamp the plywood strip in place and allow to dry thoroughly before proceeding. (FIG. 5.)

By gluing one end of the strip in place first and allowing it to dry, it will form a solid anchor as we do the rest of the bending. Still, it's a good idea to leave at least one set of clamps in place as you begin the process of gluing the rest of strip, as in Fig. 6. Apply glue to the curved edges of the house sides, then wrap the strip around the house. You'll need to remove those first clamps temporarily as you near the end of the strip, but put them back in place as you complete the bend. Add another set of clamps on the other end once you finish the wrap, and allow the completed assembly to dry.

When dry, add a ½" × ½" × 4½" square brace to the front of the helmet, as in Fig. 7. Then add a second brace, this one beveled at a 45°, to the back of the helmet. Glue these in securely, and place a single nail through each side of the helmet and into the braces. These braces not only help anchor the plywood wrapping, but also strengthen the front edges of the plywood. Note that I've left the clamps in place when adding the braces for an extra measure of security.

When the entire assembly is thoroughly dry, remove the clamps and trim the plywood overhang with a fine-cut saw or sharp utility knife, then sand everything flush as in Fig. 8. Drill a 1⅛" entry hole in the front of the house, just under the front edge of the helmet.

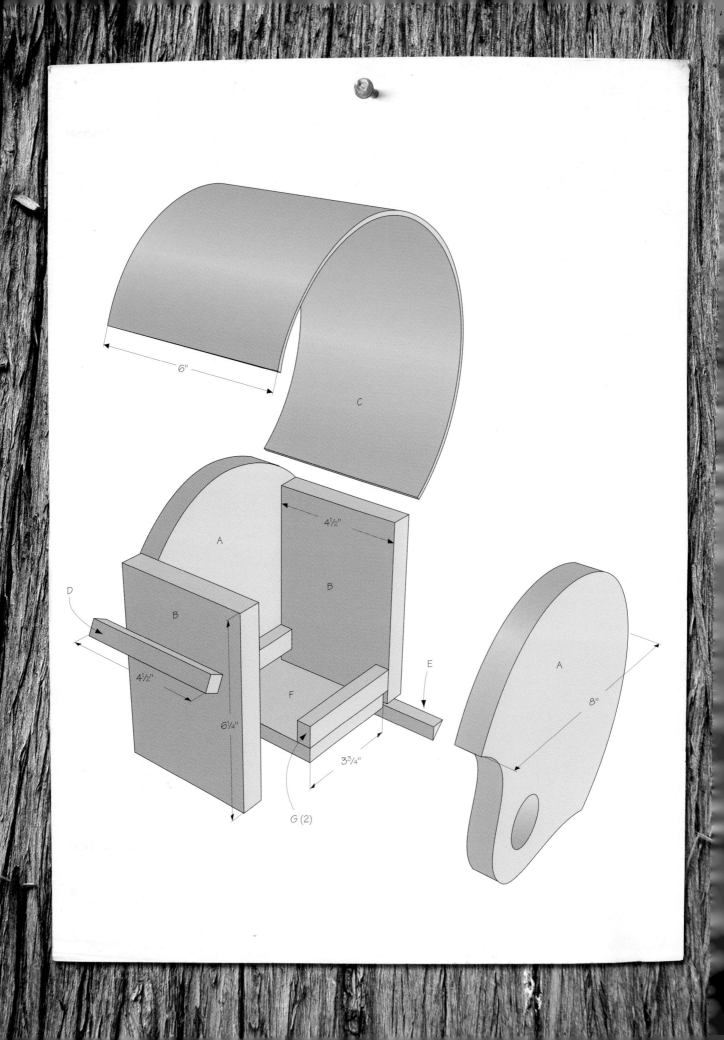

HELMET HOUSE • inches (millimeters)

REFERENCE	QUANTITY	PART	STOCK	THICKNESS	(mm)	WIDTH	(mm)	LENGTH	(mm)	COMMENTS
A	2	sides	pine	$^3/_4$	19	8	203	$8^1/_2$	216	
B	2	front/back	pine	$^3/_4$	19	$4^1/_2$	114	$6^1/_8$	155	
C	1	bent outside cover	plywood	$^1/_{16}$	2	6	12	$16^1/_2$	419	
D	1	front brace	pine	$^1/_2$	13	$^1/_2$	13	$4^1/_2$	114	
E	1	rear brace/45°	pine	$^1/_2$	13	$^1/_2$	13	$4^1/_2$	114	
F	1	bottom/door	plywood	$^1/_2$	13	$3^3/_4$	95	$4^1/_2$	114	
G	2	bottom supports	pine	$^1/_2$	13	$^3/_4$	19	4	102	

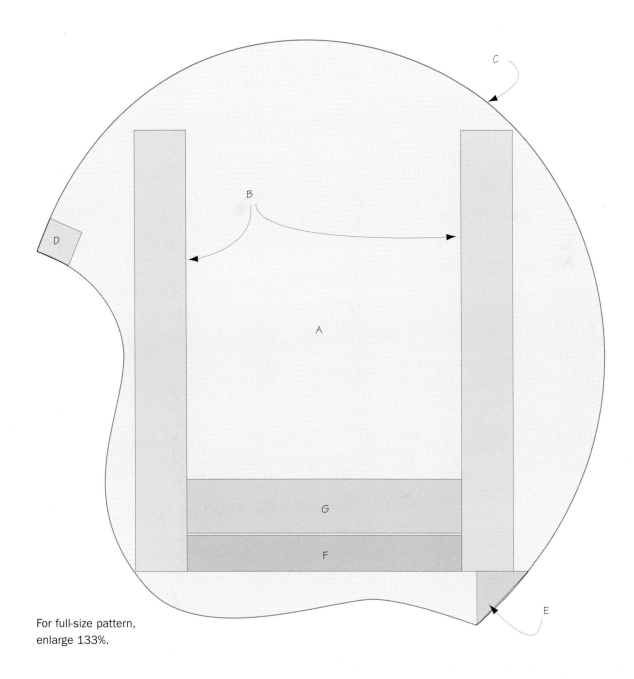

For full-size pattern,
enlarge 133%.

Prepare the house bottom, which also functions as an access door, by drilling pilot holes for the hinge. Now, glue door supports on each side and clamp these in place until dry. (Fig. 9.) Attach the house bottom and hinge, and add a screw to each side to keep the door solidly closed as in Fig. 10. This is also a good time to attach whatever means of mounting you prefer to the underside of the house. I've elected to use a copper cap, as described in Part One of this book, which will fit over a 1½" post. You can also hang the house by drilling a mounting hole or attaching a hanging hooking on one side if you prefer.

Take extra care that all plywood edges are thoroughly sealed with primer and then paint the house.

Decorate your helmet house in your favorite team colors or team logo decals. I've gone with a generic theme and opted to use ⅛" plywood to create a shooting star design that I glued to the house and then painted. I've simulated the helmet's ear-hole by drilling a shallow 1⅛" hole on each side. Masking tape helped me paint the perfectly straight yellow stripe around the center of the helmet.

FIGURE 1 The first thing you want to do is roll the plywood strip up and clamp it. This will help "set" the bend into the plywood.

FIGURE 2 A disc sander is perfect for the convex edges, while the oscillating spindle sander (shown above) is perfect for the concave curves.

FIGURE 3 There will be small gaps at the top — a very tiny gap on the back, and about ¼" at the front. These will provide ventilation for the house.

FIGURE 4 Before attaching the other side, use a square to check that all edges of the sides align perfectly with each other. Then attach the second side.

FIGURE 5 Glue just the first inch or so of the plywood in place. Let the glue dry.

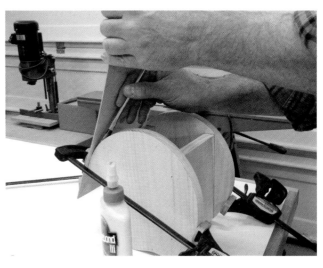

FIGURE 6 Apply glue to the curved edges of the sides and wrap the plywood around the house.

FIGURE 7 Install the square brace at the front of the house. Then install the beveled brace at the back of the helmet.

FIGURE 8 After cutting off the overhanging plywood, sand everything flush.

FIGURE 9 Glue the door supports on each side and clamp these in place until the glue is dry.

FIGURE 10 Attach the house bottom and hinge, and add a screw to each side to keep the door solidly closed.

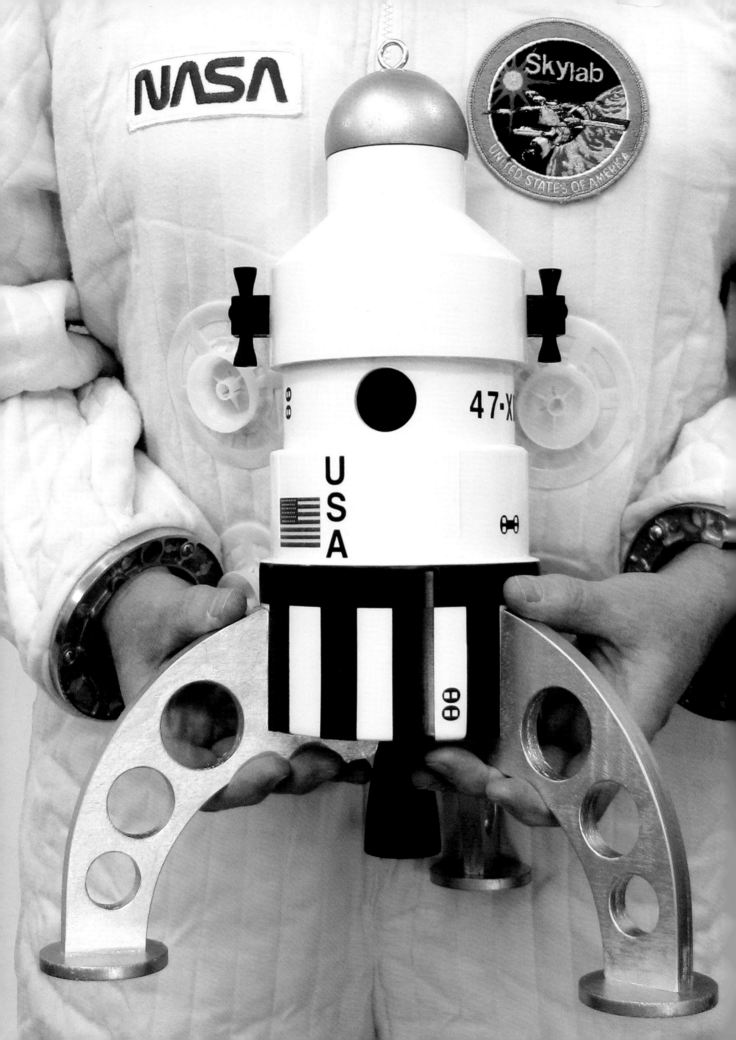

rocket house

EASILY THE MOST UNUSUAL BIRDHOUSE SO FAR in this collection, this project consists mostly of PVC components from your local home center. When it comes to decorating and customizing the appearance, with common items from your local craft or hobby store the sky is literally the limit.

The basic house shape is made of three PVC parts. The rocket base (you can consider this the first "stage" of the rocket, if you will) is a 4" × 4" soil pipe adapter, while the upper command module is a standard 4" × 2" coupling. It's important to note that the actual working dimensions of these two parts don't match their descriptions – the large opening of the soil pipe adapter is actually 5", while the opening of the small end of the coupling is 2⅜". We'll take these actual dimensions into consideration later in the project, but when at your home center look for the dimensions 4" × 4" and 4" × 2". The center component making up the rocket fuselage is a standard 4" foam-core PVC pipe, the same one we used in the pipe house earlier in the book.

Begin by cutting the fuselage to its 5" length with a handsaw, jigsaw or band saw. As I warned in the earlier pipe house chapter, do not attempt to cut PVC on a table saw. Remove any printing on the pipe with mineral spirits or alcohol, then wipe with a water-dampened rag to remove residual alcohol. The house shown here is sized for wrens and chickadees, so I've drilled a 1⅛" hole in the center of the pipe, followed by scoring the inside of the pipe below the entry hole with a rotary tool. (You can see this procedure in the pipe house chapter)

Before connecting the PVC parts, make a tracing of the inside of the large opening in the base and the small opening at the top of the command module, and use these tracings to cut out the ¾"-thick wooden inserts we'll need later.

To connect the three plastic components you'll need both primer and cement made specifically for PVC, often sold in a kit containing a can of each with applicator swabs attached to the lids. With your work area well ventilated, swab a small amount of primer onto the mating surfaces of each pipe joint according to package directions, as in Fig. 1. Be very careful with this stuff; put newspaper or other material down on your work surface and have a rag handy. And don't get it on your skin or you'll have a heck of a time getting it off. (Don't ask me how I know this.) Now swab cement on the freshly primed surface, but because we're not making these joints for plumbing purposes you don't need a lot of cement here. Just enough to seal the joint sufficiently to keep water from leaking is best. While the glue is still fresh, slide the parts together with a twisting motion until they are seated. PVC cement sets pretty quickly so do only one joint at a time, working quickly but carefully.

At this point, the main portion of the rocket is complete. Depending on the brand of PVC couplings you get, they may have embossed lettering on them. If so, this can easily be sanded off. Be sure the last sanding you do is with very fine sandpaper for a smooth finish.

Sandwich three pieces of ½" plywood together, then transfer the pattern for the landing struts to the combined workpiece. I made my workpieces a bit longer on the ends and used brads to hold them together. Cut the curves of the landing struts, but don't cut to length. With them still attached together, mark the locations for the holes as in Fig. 2, then drill through all three pieces at the same time. Sand the outside edges of the struts – the convex edges can be smoothed on a disc sander or with a hand-held sander, while a spindle sander is perfect for the concave edges and holes as shown in Fig. 3. With your sanding complete, cut the combined workpieces to length, separating the individual struts.

Drill a pilot hole through the center of the floor, and attach the rocket engine cone. I made the engine with a 3½" "wooden doll body" (available at most craft supply stores) by cutting off the rounded top and sanding the bottom smooth. Drill a pilot hole into the top of the engine and attach it to the house floor with glue and a single screw as in Fig. 4.

To attach the landing struts, first mount the floor insert into the rocket base with three evenly-spaced exterior screws set into countersunk pilot holes drilled through the base sides. Now upend the rocket and drill a pair of pilot holes through each strut and into the underside of the rocket floor. Using glue along with round-head screws and washers, attach the struts to the rocket as in Fig 5. It's important to use round-head screws and washers here, as the angled heads of flat-head screws would split the plywood when tightened. Now, drill pilot holes into the landing feet and the bottoms of the struts, and use glue and screws to attach the feet. Finally, drill a few ¼" or ⅜" holes into the floor for drainage and ventilation. Attached to the house with screws, the entire landing-gear assembly can be removed to clean the house.

Moving to top of the rocket, cut a 3" hardwood ball (available from any craft store) in half, then glue and screw it to the top insert we cut earlier. Attach this to the top of the command module with a pair of counter-sunk screws through the sides. If you plan to hang your house, add a screw eye to the top.

At this point, all that's left is painting and decorating the rocket. Detach the landing assembly, fill and sand any plywood voids, then seal the entire assembly, except for the inner surfaces of the floor insert, with a good primer before painting. Repeat for the rocket top.

To create the maneuvering thrusters on the command module, I drilled holes through a pair of ¾" hardwood cubes. I then marked and cut sections of hard-wood spindle to make the thruster cones, then glued them into the holes in the cubes as in Fig. 6. To make the cubes fit securely to the rounded side of the command module, wrap a piece of sandpaper around the PVC pipe then rub the thruster assembly across the sandpaper until the underside takes on a curved shape matching the side of the PVC. Prime and paint the assemblies, then affix them to the side of the command module with epoxy.

The various markings were easy. The familiar black-and-white striping (which the NASA folks call a roll pattern) is black vinyl tape. The American flag is a vinyl peel-off sticker. The lettering came from a sheet of vinyl peel-off letters, while those little markings that look like vents came from the same sheet — they're the normally unused center portions of the letters. And, if you're really ambitious, you can scavenge all sorts of high-tech-looking gadgetry from plastic model kits that you can attach in a variety of ways for an authentic out-of-this-world appearance.

FIGURE 1 Swab a small amount of primer onto the mating surfaces of each pipe joint according to package directions.

FIGURE 2 Cut the curves of the landing struts, but don't cut them to length yet. With them still attached together, mark the locations for the holes, then drill through all three pieces at the same time.

FIGURE 3 The convex edges can be smoothed on a disc sander or with a hand-held sander, while a spindle sander is perfect for the concave edges and holes.

ROCKET HOUSE • inches (millimeters)

REFERENCE	QUANTITY	PART	STOCK	THICKNESS	(mm)	WIDTH	(mm)	LENGTH	(mm)	COMMENTS
A	1	rocket base	PVC adapter			4 d	102	4	102	
B	1	rocket fuselage	PVC			4 d	102	5	127	
C	1	command module	PVC coupling			4 d	102	2	51	
D	1	floor insert	pine	$3/4$	19	5 d	127			
E	1	rocket engine (a)	hardwood	$1^1/2$	38	$2^3/8$ d	60			
F	3	landing strut	plywood	$1/2$	13	$5^7/8$	149	$6^1/8$	156	
G	1	top insert	pine	$3/4$	19	$2^3/8$ d	60			
H	1	top	hardwood ball			3 d	76			
I	3	landing feet	hardwood disc	$1/4$	6	$2^3/8$ d	60			
J	2	thruster assembly (b)	hardwood	$3/4$	19	$3/4$	19	$3/4$	19	

a - A $3^1/2$" "Wooden Doll Body" from a craft supply store, with top cut off and bottom sanded flat.

b - Thruster assembly consists of $3/4$" hardwood cube with cut sections of hardwood spindle glued into drilled holes. See main project text.

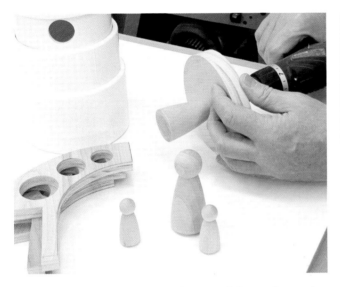

FIGURE 4 Drill a pilot hole into the top of the engine and attach it to the house floor with glue and a single screw.

FIGURE 5 Using glue, along with round-head screws and washers, attach the struts to the rocket.

FIGURE 6 Mark and cut sections of hardwood spindle to make the thruster cones, then glue them into the holes in the cubes.

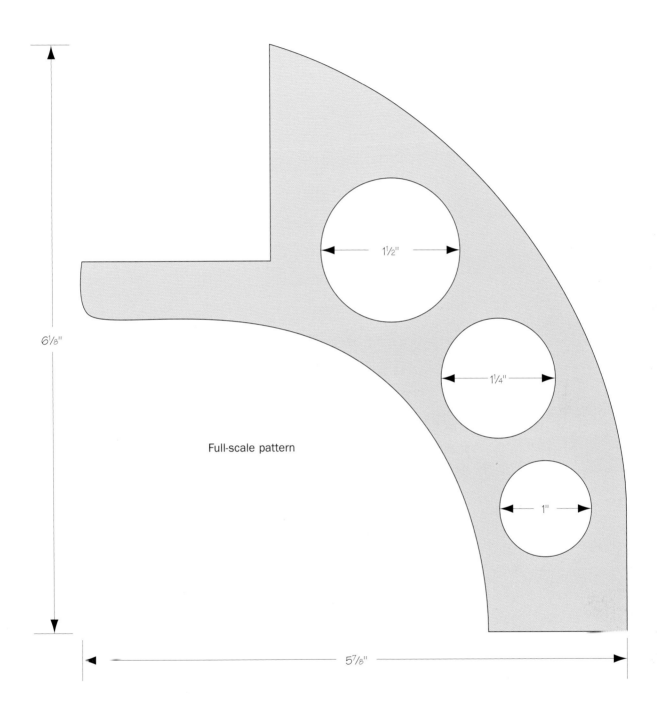

Full-scale pattern

6⅛"

5⅞"

1½"

1¼"

1"

the old woman's shoe

"THERE WAS AN OLD WOMAN WHO LIVED IN a shoe..." Well, you know the rest. And if an old woman (along with an unspecified number of children) could live in a shoe, I can't think of any reason why birds couldn't.

Made with a combination of solid pine and thin plywood, this project's construction is straightforward but does require some final shaping that takes a bit of time and care to complete. Like the helmet birdhouse a few projects back, you'll be bending $1/16$" plywood, so begin this project by cutting the shoe front, making sure that the surface grain of the plywood runs side-to-side. To make clamping easier, it's best to cut this piece slightly oversize; it can be easily trimmed later. As we did with the helmet birdhouse, it's a good idea to pre-shape the plywood, and you can see in Fig. 1 that I simplified the process by placing the workpiece inside a scrap of PVC pipe and clamping the ends. When it comes time to use this piece later during construction, it should be nicely curved.

Cut the components for the house sides, back and center wall. We'll cut the roof angles and the overall shoe shape later in the construction, so leave these components straight-sided for now. Create the shoe's toe block by gluing up three pieces of $3/4$" × 4" × 3" pine and clamping till dry. Note that the grain of these pieces should run in the direction of the short dimension. While the toe block is drying, use the main shoe pattern as a guide to transfer the locations for the house back and center wall to the shoe sides to aid placement, as in Fig. 2, then glue and nail them in place to one side of the house only. (Fig. 3.)

Glue the toe block into the front of the shoe as shown in Fig. 4, and clamp. When the assembly is dry, glue and nail the other side of the shoe in place. (Fig. 5.) Be very careful with your nail placement, and avoid nailing in any area that will be shaped later, especially near the front edges.

When the assembly is dry, head to the band saw to begin shaping the shoe, starting with the shoe profile.

With the shoe on its side, carefully follow the outline of the shoe sides on both the front and back of the house. (Fig. 6.) Now sand the profile smooth. A disc sander works best for the convex shape on the shoe toe, while a spindle sander easily handles the concave areas, as in Fig. 7. Now head back to the band saw again to round off the toe sides; this time hold the shoe vertically and round just the toe corners. Follow once again with sanding to smooth out the toe shape. At this point, leave all edges square; we'll do final sanding and rounding a bit later, but all edges must remain sharp and square until the shoe front and side quarters have been attached.

Position the $1/16$" plywood shoe front so that it overlaps the top center wall, then glue and clamp in place until dry, as in Fig. 8.

While this assembly is drying, prepare the shoe quarters. Throughout this book, whenever possible I've cut identical components at the same time by making them a bit oversized and nailing or gluing them together at the waste edges, then cutting them out. For the shoe quarters I took the two workpieces and stacked them on top of a third. This scrap piece on the bottom will help prevent the thin plywood from tearing out on the undersides of the quarters when cut and drilled. Use the shoe quarter pattern to transfer the component outline to your stack and cut them out on all edges except the top so they stay together. Now drill the shoelace holes as indicated on the front edge. (Fig. 9.) Finally, make the last cut on the top of the stack to free the individual quarters. Again, no need to cut these to shape at the top yet; everything will be trimmed at the same time when cutting the roof angles.

Glue and clamp the shoe quarters in place on each side of the shoe. When dry, cut out the top roof angles on the band saw, as in Fig. 10. Cut the top $3/8$" to $1/2$" off the tip of the roof crown on the back of the house to create a ventilation opening. Add a $3/4$" × $3/4$" × 4" brace to the inside of the shoe at the top edge of the thin front by gluing the piece in place so that the top edge of the brace extends beyond the roof angle you just cut. When the brace is dry, use the band saw to trim it flush with the roof angle at the front.

Add the entrance hole ring by gluing and clamping a hardwood disc to the house front about 2" on-center from the roof crown. When dry, drill a 1⅛" entrance hole (suitable for wrens and chickadees) through the center of the disc, creating a round window effect.

I've given the roof a 100° crown. To make the roof, bevel the top edges of the roof halves at 50°. Apply a piece of wide tape to the back edges of the roof joint, spread glue into the joint and fold the roof using the tape as a "hinge." When dry, glue and nail the roof in place atop the house, as in Fig. 11. With the main house now complete, feel free to do some final sanding to round over all edges except the bottom, which should fit flush on the sole.

To create the shoe sole, which serves as the floor of the house, trace your shoe's shape onto a piece of ¾" stock, making the sole about ⅛" larger all around. To simulate the heel, make a vertical cut halfway through the bottom of the sole 3" from the back (the cut should be ⅜" deep). Angle a second cut toward the front of the sole. Now refine the shape of the sole bottom with a

sander, as in Fig. 12. Drill four countersunk pilot holes through the bottom of the sole and up into the underside of the house, and attach the sole with 1¼" exterior screws. Finally, drill a few ¼" or ⅜" drainage holes through the bottom.

You can decorate your shoe house any way you wish, but remember to fill edge voids on the plywood parts, and seal everything with a good coat of primer before painting. You an create windows from scratch by gluing up individual pieces (you'll see this method in the cottage birdhouse later in this section), but you can shorten the process by taking the easy shortcut I took. I picked up some plywood house cutouts (about 20 cents each at a craft supply store), and then simply cut the windows out as in Fig. 13. For the door, I glued one of these window cutouts to a rectangular piece of thin plywood, then glued the door assembly to the house.

Other touches to consider might include a chimney, cedar shingles, or even a TV antenna. (Or, if your old woman is high-tech, a small satellite dish.) Don't forget your shoelace; you'll need a shoelace – or any thin cord – of at least 72" to lace it up and tie it. Be sure to tie the shoelace tightly, or you might find it used for nest building.

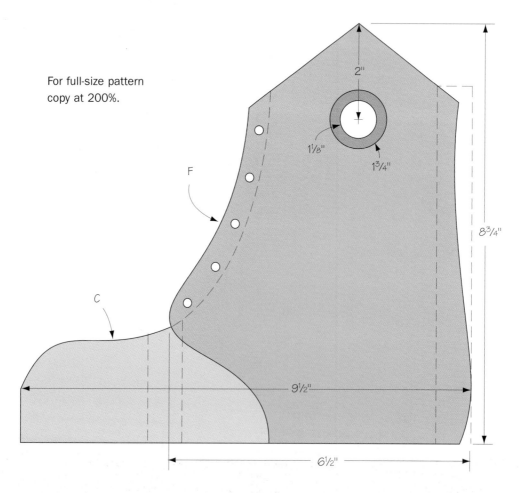

For full-size pattern copy at 200%.

THE OLD WOMAN'S SHOE • inches (millimeters)

REFERENCE	QUANTITY	PART	STOCK	THICKNESS	(mm)	WIDTH	(mm)	LENGTH	(mm)	COMMENTS
A	1	back (a)	pine	$3/4$	19	4	102	$8^3/_4$	222	
B	1	center wall (b)	pine	$3/4$	19	4	102	3	76	
C	2	shoe sides	pine	$1/2$	13	$9^1/_2$	241	$8^3/_4$	222	
D	1	toe (b)	pine	$2^1/_4$	57	4	102	3	76	
E	1	shoe front (c)	plywood	$1/16$	2	5	127	8	203	
F	2	shoe quarters (a)	plywood	$1/8$	3	$6^1/_2$	165	$8^3/_4$	222	
G	2	roof	pine	$1/2$	13	4	102	$6^1/_2$	165	
H	1	shoe sole	pine	$3/4$	19	$5^1/_2$	140	10	254	
I	1	hole ring	hardwood disc	$3/16$	5	$1^3/_4$ d	45			
J	1	upper brace	pine	$3/4$	19	$3/4$	19	4	102	

a - Height of shoe side is $8^3/_4$", but this piece will be trimmed when shoe is shaped.

b - This piece will be trimmed when shoe is shaped.

c - The 8" length of this piece allows clamping room, and will be trimmed when shoe is shaped. It's best to make this piece about $1/4$" wider on each side to facilitate clamping.

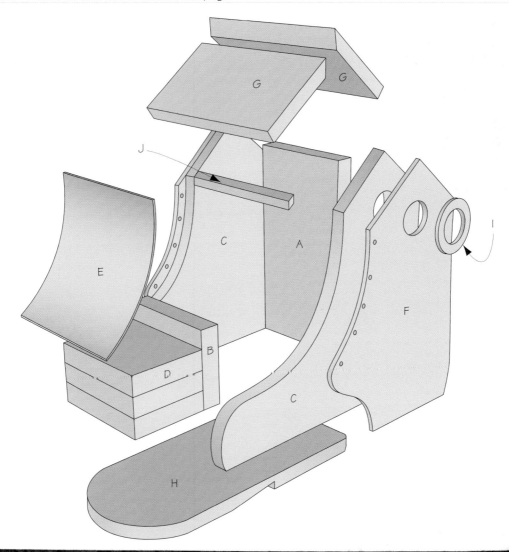

FIGURE 1 It's a good idea to pre-shape the plywood.

FIGURE 2 Use the main shoe pattern as a guide to transfer the locations for the house back and center wall to the shoe sides.

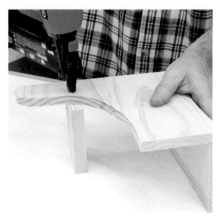

FIGURE 3 Glue and nail them in place to one side of the house only.

FIGURE 4 Glue the toe block into the front of the shoe.

FIGURE 5 Glue and nail the other side of the shoe in place.

FIGURE 6 With the shoe on its side, carefully follow the outline of the shoe sides on both the front and back of the house.

FIGURE 7 A disc sander works best for the convex shape on the shoe toe, while a spindle sander easily handles the concave areas

FIGURE 8 Position the 1/16" plywood shoe front so that it overlaps the top center wall, then glue and clamp in place until dry.

FIGURE 9 Drill the shoelace holes as indicated on the front edge.

FIGURE 10 When dry, cut out the top roof angles on the band saw.

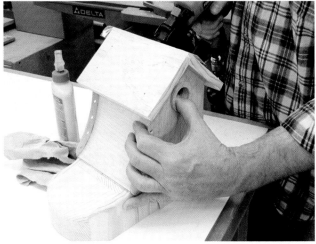

FIGURE 11 Apply a piece of wide tape to the back edges of the roof joint, spread glue into the joint and fold the roof using the tape as a "hinge." Glue and nail the roof in place atop the house.

FIGURE 12 Refine the shape of the sole bottom with a sander.

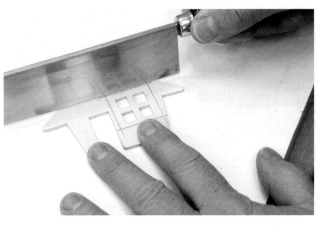

FIGURE 13 I cut the windows out of plywood house shapes found at a local crafts store.

outhouse

HERE'S A TOUCH OF WHIMSY THAT FITS WELL in any garden or backyard. Styled like a classic country outhouse, right down to the traditional crescent-moon entrance hole, this project will bring smiles to your family and become a welcome home for wrens and chickadees. (Even if they don't get the joke.)

If the basic construction looks familiar, it should — essentially it's a reworking of the swallow house from an earlier chapter, but the major components are given a 180° spin to reflect the backward slanting roofline common to outhouses. Old barn wood would be a good choice for this birdhouse if you have a source of it. I didn't, so I simulated old wood with the roughest ¾" cedar I could find, then gave it a wash coat of thinned gray paint for a weathered appearance.

For a more slanted appearance, I've opted for a steeper roof angle instead than usual. When cutting the components, the house sides should be angled 15° at the tops, while the top of the front/door, the house back and the rear edge of the roof should be beveled at 15°. Take care when cutting your angles and bevels to do them so the rough side of the cedar will be oriented outward for each component. Since the smooth face of your cedar faces inward, be sure to create a climbable surface on the inside of the door/front by roughing or grooving, or attaching a bit of wire mesh.

Begin by attaching the house back to the sides with glue and nails as in Fig. 1. Temporarily clamp the front/door in place so the house remains square, then flip the house over and attach the plywood floor so that the rear edge is flush with the back of the house as in Fig. 2.

In keeping with the rustic look of the outhouse, I rounded each edge of the house a bit more than I usually do, especially on both edges of the door/front and the edges of the front opening as in Fig. 3. For most of the houses in this book with pivoting sides or fronts for access the door isn't apparent, but for the outhouse you'll want the front to be an obvious door. Rounding the edges with a sanding block will give the desired effect.

Draw the pattern for the entry hole on the front/door, centered about 6½" above the floor. (This is a bit higher than I usually do entrance holes for wrens, but they won't care.) You can cut the opening out with a jigsaw, but I opted for a coping saw. (Fig. 4.) In either case, start by drilling a small hole near one edge of the pattern as a starting point for the saw blade. Because the entrance is elongated, you'll note that the pattern is only 1" at its widest point. Wrens and chickadees will navigate it easily.

Line up the rear edge of the roof with the outhouse back, and attach it with glue and nails. Test fit the door/front, and sand or plane the sides so it pivots smoothly in the opening. Drive a galvanized finish nail through each side about 1" down from the top for the pivot hinges. As always, measure your nail locations carefully on each side. With the door in place there will be an approximate ¼" gap at the top that will provide ventilation and allow the door to pivot freely without rubbing at the top as in Fig. 5. Now, drill an angled hole on one side near the bottom and slip in a galvanized nail to secure the door. Finally, drill a few ¼" or ⅜" drainage holes through the bottom of the house.

Cedar will naturally take on a weathered silver-gray patina with age, but I gave the outhouse a time-worn appearance with a painted wash coat. Mix exterior latex-based gray paint with water until translucent, and then give the house a single coat. The wash coat adds a weathered gray color, but allows the grain and natural wood color to show through.

FIGURE 1 Attach the house back to the sides with glue and nails.

FIGURE 2 Attach the plywood floor so that the rear edge is flush with the back of the house.

FIGURE 3 Round over the edges of the parts more than usual. This helps with the weathered look.

FIGURE 4 Either a jigsaw or coping saw will work for cutting out the entrance hole.

FIGURE 5 With the door in place there will be an approximate ¼" gap at the top that will provide ventilation and allow the door to pivot freely without rubbing at the top.

OUTHOUSE • inches (millimeters)

REFERENCE	QUANTITY	PART	STOCK	THICKNESS	(mm)	WIDTH	(mm)	LENGTH	(mm)	COMMENTS
A	1	front/door	cedar	¾	19	4	102	9¾	248	
B	2	sides	cedar	¾	19	5½	140	10	254	
C	1	back	cedar	¾	19	5½	140	8½	216	
D	1	bottom	plywood	½	13	6	152	7	178	
E	1	roof	cedar	¾	19	5½	140	7	178	

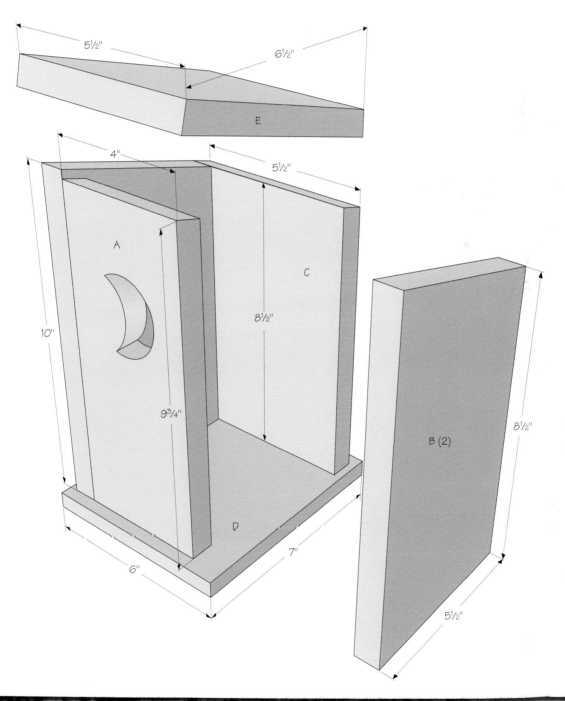

lighthouse

LIGHTHOUSES COME IN A DIZZYING ARRAY OF sizes, types, styles and construction methods. Among the quaintest are the all-wood lighthouses common on large lakes, bays and inlets. Their angular shapes also lend themselves well to easy-to-construct birdhouses. This particular house is based on an actual lighthouse in Hampton, Nova Scotia. However, I've taken the liberty of enlarging the scale a bit and added an attached lightkeeper's house to the light tower (the original lighthouse has only a doorway entrance).

This house mixes several materials — ¾" and ½" pine, ⅛" and ½" plywood, ⅜" hardwood dowels, a ³⁄₁₆" hardwood disc and 2" plastic tubing. Paint in your choice of colors completes the lighthouse for a realistic and attractive appearance.

I've divided the project into three sections, which all come together to make the birdhouse. The first section is the main tower, started by cutting the four sides to length from a 5½"-wide piece of ½" stock as in Fig. 1. Bevel the tops and bottoms of the tower sides at 10° so that, once assembled, both top and bottom of the tower will be flat. Transfer the outline for the four sides to your workpieces using the pattern provided. Note that two of the tower sides, although identical in shape, are 1" narrower than the other pair. This will offset the dimensions of the wider sides when joined, forming a perfectly square tower.

When adding an entrance ring to a painted birdhouse, I like to attach the ring early in the process. This assures that once primed and painted, all edges are sealed, helping to prevent moisture from creeping underneath the ring. Glue a ³⁄₁₆" hardwood disc 1¾" in diameter to the front of the tower, centered about 5" from the bottom. To apply even clamping pressure, use a flat piece of scrap between the clamp and the disc, as in Fig. 2. This house is sized for wrens and chickadees, so when the glue is dry remove the clamp and drill a 1⅛" hole in the disc center.

Assemble the house with waterproof glue and nails

as in Fig. 3. Note here how the narrow sides fit between the wider front and back.

With the tower complete, set it aside and cut out the front and back of the lightkeeper's house according to the illustrations. Because we're working with small pieces here, I found it easier to cut the two sides of the lightkeeper's house to width, but leave them a bit long for now, not bothering with the roof bevel yet. Assemble the house with glue and clamps only as in Fig. 4. When the assembly is dry, use a band saw or handsaw to trim the tops of those side pieces to match the 45° slope of the little house's roofline.

To make the lightkeeper's house fit flush against the main tower, cut the back of the house at a 10° angle as in Fig. 5. Sand the back of the house smooth to create a tight joint, and glue it in place against the side of the main tower. While this assembly is drying, cut the two ⅛"-thick roof pieces to size and angle the rear edge of each half to match the slope of the main tower. Glue the roof halves into place, securing them with a few very fine nails of pins. The lightkeeper house and tower assembly is now complete.

The top section of the lighthouse has a ¾"-thick floor piece, and a 2¼"-thick roof piece. Make the roof by laminating three pieces of ¾" pine with waterproof glue, and clamp up till dry. When dry, trim the resulting block as needed to its 3½" × 3½" dimensions. Drill a 2" hole ⅜" deep in the center of the top floor and top roof workpieces as in Fig. 6. Now, drill ⅜" dowel holes all the way through the four corners of the floor, and ⅜" deep into the underside of roof. (If you clamp these two pieces together, you can drill the holes at the same time to ensure that the holes are perfectly aligned. Just be sure to set your drill stop so the holes in the roof go no deeper than ⅜".)

Draw cut lines on all four sides of the roof, extending from ¾" from the bottom up to the center on each side. On the band saw, carefully cut the roof angles first

LIGHTHOUSE • inches (millimeters)

REFERENCE	QUANTITY	PART	STOCK	THICKNESS	(mm)	WIDTH	(mm)	LENGTH	(mm)	COMMENTS
A	2	tower front/back	pine	1/2	13	5 1/2	140	8	203	
B	2	tower sides	pine	1/2	13	4 1/2	115	8	203	
C	2	keeper house front/back	pine	1/2	13	3	76	4	102	
D	2	keeper house sides	pine	1/2	13	1 3/4	45	3 1/8	79	
E	1	keeper house right roof	plywood	1/8	3	2 3/8	61	3 1/2	89	
F	1	keeper house left roof	plywood	1/8	3	2 1/2	64	3 1/2	89	
G	1	lighthouse top, floor	pine	3/4	19	3 1/2	89	3 1/2	89	
H	1	lighthouse top, roof	pine	2 1/4	57	3 1/2	89	3 1/2	89	
J	1	entrance ring	disc	3/16	5	1 3/4 d	45			
K	1	bottom	plywood	1/2	13	5 1/2	140	9	229	
L	4	roof posts	dowel	3/8	10	2 3/4 d	70			
M	4	railing	plywood	1/8	3	7/8	22	2 1/2	64	
N	1	light "glass"	plastic tube	1/16	2	2	51	2 3/4 d	70	

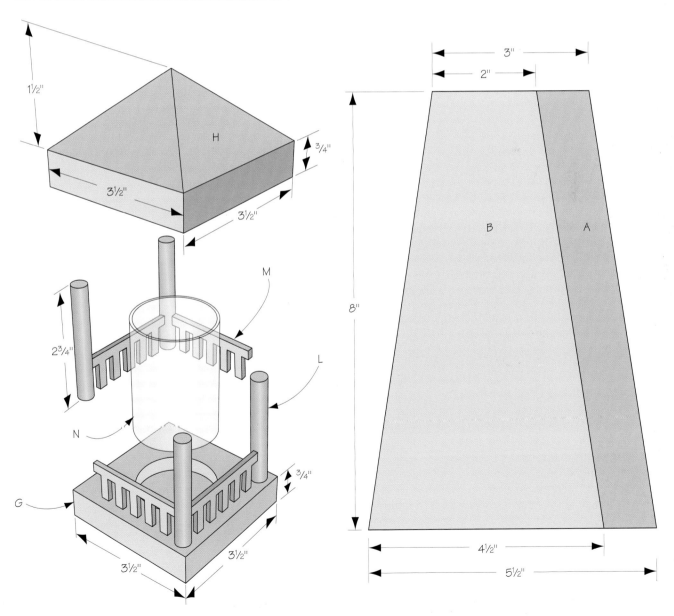

on one side, then flip it over and cut the roof angle on the opposite side. Now, use masking tape or clear packing tape to reattach the two pieces you just cut off. This will give you two flat surfaces to cut the other two sides, as in Fig. 7. It's fine to cut right through the tape, but do this operation very slowly and carefully. When done, you now have a four-sided roof piece. Sand each face smooth.

Prepare the lighthouse "glass" by cutting a 2¾" piece of plastic tubing. I used the same 2"-diameter tubing from the Finch Feeder project, but you can use any size. Just be sure to alter the project dimensions and the size of the two large holes to accommodate the tubing you use. I didn't want a completely clear glass, so I scuffed the inside of the tubing with some steel wool, but you skip this if you prefer. Glue the four dowels in place into the roof as in Fig. 8 and allow to dry. Paint the components of the top before assembly, taking care not to get paint in the holes in the floor corners, or on the bottom tips of the dowels. When the paint is dry, slip the tube into the floor piece. Put glue into the floor holes and lower the roof onto the floor, sliding the dowels into place. Slide the roof down firmly until it stops, holding the tubing snugly in place. This is why I drilled the dowel holes all the way through the bottom piece, to account for slight variances of cutting the tube or drilling the top dowel holes. If the dowels protrude through the bottom of the floor, just sand them flush when the glue dries.

I made the railings for the lighthouse top using ⅛" plywood picket fence from a dollhouse supply store, trimming the fence with a fine-cut saw as in Fig. 9. Dry-fit each piece as you make them, but don't glue them on yet. After cutting the four railings to size, you may find it easier to paint the back side of them now, as it would be difficult to do so once they're glued in place. Attach the lighthouse top to the main assembly with glue and fine nails or pins. With the top in place, glue on the four railings and paint as necessary.

Now, attach the entire assembly to the base, driving four screws up through the bottom and into the assembly. A few ¼" or ⅜" holes drilled through the base provide drainage and ventilation.

For a final touch, I added windows (also cut from that dollhouse picket fence) and a door to the lightkeeper's house.

FIGURE 1 Cut the four sides to length.

FIGURE 2 Use a flat piece of scrap between the clamp and the disc.

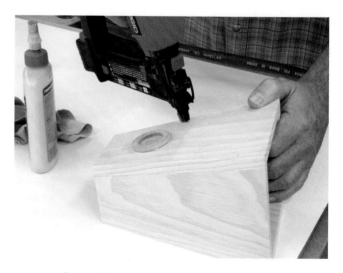

FIGURE 3 Assemble the house with waterproof glue and nails.

FIGURE 4 Assemble the house with glue and clamps only.

FIGURE 5 Cut the back of the house at a 10° angle to fit flush against the main tower.

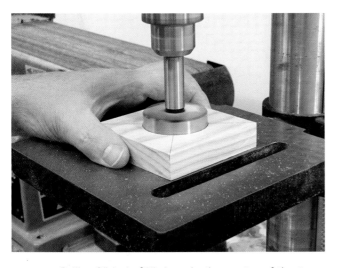

FIGURE 6 Drill a 2" hole ⅜" deep in the center of the top floor and top roof workpieces.

FIGURE 7 Use masking tape or clear packing tape to reattach the two pieces you just cut off. This will give you two flat surfaces to cut the other two sides.

FIGURE 8 Glue the four dowels in place into the roof and allow to dry.

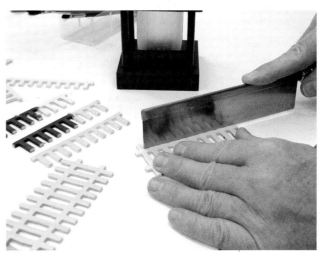

FIGURE 9 I made the railings for the lighthouse top using ⅛" plywood picket fence from a dollhouse supply store.

house trailer birdhouse

FOR MANY FAMILIES IN THE 1950s AND 1960s, part of the American dream was to own a small trailer. Towed behind the family car, a small trailer gave the freedom to go anywhere and still be close to "home." This project takes the style of a 1950's trailer and gives it a feathered spin.

Although there are a lot of parts, this trailer birdhouse is simpler than it looks because the basic house is still a box of six components — front, back, top, bottom and two sides. I've used a mix of ¾" pine and ½" plywood, along with assorted dowels, discs and wheels from the local craft store. Once again, I've sized this house and entry hole for wrens, but resize it for other birds as you wish.

Cut out the components per the cut list, but keep in mind that several of the parts will be further worked and shaped. The bottom of the trailer, of ½" plywood, serves as both the house floor and door for cleaning, so start there. Cut the bottom to width and mark where the front will go; from there draw angled lines toward the front edge as in Fig. 1, then trim the corners off with a hand- or power saw. Now construct the main box of the house using glue only, no nails. In Fig. 2 I've put the bottom in place as I clamped up the box, helping to achieve a square glueup. (Take care not to get glue on the bottom piece.)

When the glue has dried, unclamp the assembly and set the bottom aside for now. Transfer the outlines for the side pattern to the workpieces, and glue and nail them in place on the box, being sure to place the nails sufficiently inside the pattern outline that they won't be in the way for the next step. Allow the glue to dry, then cut out the pattern on the band saw as in Fig. 3.

Turn the house upside down and put the bottom/door in place. Attach the bottom to the rear of the house with a pair of small hinges. (Fig. 4) I used brass hinges measuring ¾" × 1", but any small, weather-resistant hinges will do; if you prefer, you can use a single longer hinge instead of two longer ones. Test the door when the hinges are on; if it sticks and is difficult to open, sand the edges until it works smoothly. Drill a pilot hole through the front side of the house and into the bottom/door near the front for a screw that will keep the bottom/door in place, but can be removed to pivot the bottom down for cleaning. (Just one screw is fine to keep the door closed.) Finally, drill a few ¼" holes in the bottom for drainage, and a pair on the upper back for ventilation.

With the basic bird box complete, give the outside a good sanding to remove the saw marks from the shaping process and leave everything nice and smooth for painting later. (Fig. 5)

Using the photos and drawings as a guide, attach the windows and doors with glue. In Fig. 6, I've started with the front windshield, which I made just a hair long on the ends. When the glue was dry I sanded the sides so this window was perfectly flush with the sides, and then glued the side windows into place. Once sanded and painted, these three pieces give the appearance of a continuous wraparound window.

The wheel wells start as solid 2"-diameter plywood discs glued to the trailer sides where indicated. We'll only use half of each, but leave them whole for now. When the glue is dry, use a 1½" Forstner bit to drill a ⅜"-deep hole in the center of the disks. (If your drill press has a stop, set it so the hole goes no deeper than ⅜".) You can see in Fig. 7 that by leaving the discs whole, the resulting ring acts to guide the Forstner bit accurately and safely. When the holes are done, trim off the bottom of the ring with a fine saw — or even clippers — and sand smooth. Center the wheels in the wheel wells and glue in place.

Drill a ⅜" hole into the underside of the bottom near the front, and glue the front support dowel in place. Cut two 1⅛" lengths of ¾" dowel and attach them side-by-side onto the front of the trailer to simulate a pair of propane tanks. Be sure to glue them to the front of the trailer only so the bottom/door will open

HOUSE TRAILER BIRDHOUSE • inches (millimeters)

REFERENCE	QUANTITY	PART	STOCK	THICKNESS	(mm)	WIDTH	(mm)	LENGTH	(mm)	COMMENTS
A	1	front	pine	3/4	19	4 1/2	114	6	152	
B	1	back	pine	3/4	19	4 1/2	114	6 1/2	165	
C	1	top	plywood	1/2	13	4 1/2	114	6 1/2	165	
D	1	bottom	plywood	1/2	13	4 1/2	114	8 3/4	222	
E	2	sides	plywood	1/2	13	6 1/2	165	7	178	
F	2	windows	plywood	1/8	3	1 1/2	38	2	51	
G	1	front window	plywood	1/8	3	2	51	5 1/4	133	
H	1	door	plywood	1/8	3	1 3/4	45	5	127	
I	1	small window	plywood	1/8	3	1	25	1 3/8	35	
J	1	rear window	plywood	1/8	3	1 1/4	32	3 3/4	92	
K	2	wheel well	plywood disc	1/8	3	2 d	51			
L	2	wheel	hardwood	1/2	13	1 1/2 d	38			
M	1	bumper	hardwood	3/8	10	3/8	10	14 3/4	375	
N	1	front support	dowel	1/4 d	6	1	25			
O	2	propane tanks	dowel	3/4 d	19	1 3/8	35			

Part K is a thin plywood disc. It and Part L (wheel) are available at any craft supply store.

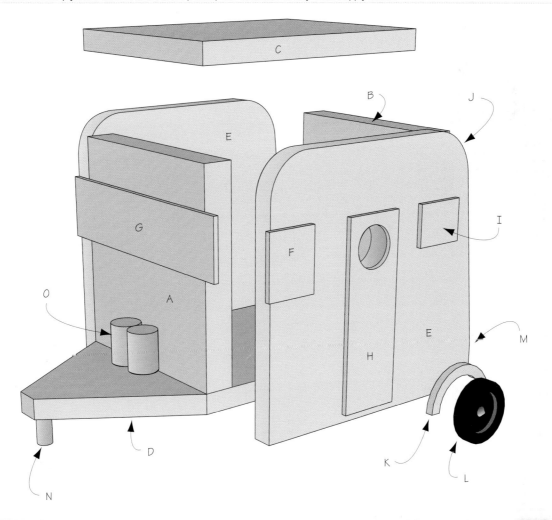

freely. Finally, add a bumper. I used a ⅜" × ⅜" strip of hardwood, which I glued and pinned to the lower back

The trailer birdhouse is now complete. Since this is a painted project, as a last step you may wish to fill your nail holes with wood filler and then sand smooth as I've done in Fig. 8. All that's left is to drill the round "window" into the door, which serves as the entry hole for the birdhouse. As this house is geared to wrens, I drilled a 1⅛" hole.

Paint your trailer any way you wish, but start with a coat of primer first. The primer will help to seal the edges and glue joints of all the glued-on trims — like windows. The last touch I made was to add a pair of round hubs to the wheels, which I painted silver.

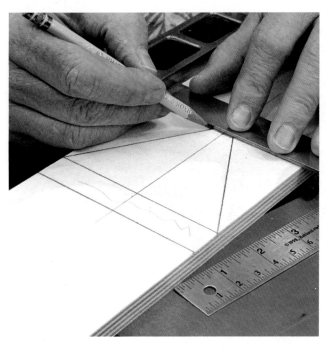

FIGURE 1 Cut the bottom to width and mark where the front will go; then draw angled lines toward the front edge.

FIGURE 2 Construct the main box of the house using glue only.

FIGURE 3 Cut out the pattern on the band saw.

FIGURE 4 Attach the bottom to the rear of the house with a pair of small hinges.

FIGURE 5 Give the outside a good sanding to remove the saw marks from the shaping process.

FIGURE 6 Attach the windows and doors with glue.

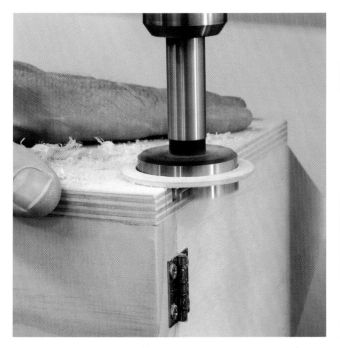

FIGURE 7 The ring acts to guide the Forstner bit accurately and safely for creating the wheel wells.

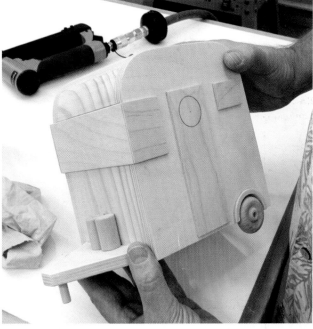

FIGURE 8 Before painting, you may wish to fill your nail holes with wood filler and then sand them smooth.

dog house

THE TYPICAL BACKYARD IS OFTEN SHARED BY not only our feathered friends, but by man's best friend. The design of this doghouse birdhouse combines two of our favorite animals into a single theme.

The construction of this doghouse is similar to the Finch House project presented earlier in the book, as well as the Cottage birdhouse coming up later in this section. Many of the components are the same and use the same 45° roof bevels, but I've sized them here to create a house for small birds like wrens. You can make this house for just about any bird by changing the size and location of the entrance hole and adjusting the components to create larger interior house dimensions.

I've opted for plywood for this house, and started by drawing the doghouse pattern onto the ¼" stock that comprises the false front of the house. (Fig. 1.) At this point, you can attach the workpieces for the false front and both the house front and back together and cut them out simultaneously. Separate the workpieces and cut the large entrance arch on the false front; also cut off the top ½" of the house back to create a ventilation hole. Now glue the false front to the main house front. Note in Fig. 2 how I've used wood blocks as clamping cauls to evenly distribute the pressure. When the glue is dry, unclamp and drill a 1⅛" entrance hole at the top edge of the arch. This will place the hole at 4" above the floor, on center.

Cut the house sides to size, beveling the top edge of each side at 45°. With waterproof glue and nails, attach the house sides to the back first, then attach the house front to the assembly. (Fig. 3.)

Attach the right roof half with glue and nails so that the top edge is even with the roof crown. Follow this with the left roof, overlapping the top edge to make a 90° joint as in Fig. 4.

Cut the house base to size. Drill four countersunk pilot holes through the base and into the house walls from underneath, then attach the base with exterior screws only, no glue. This way you can remove the base to clean the house. Lastly, drill a few ¼" or ⅜" holes through the bottom for drainage.

The house is now done and ready for priming and painting. As always, fill any plywood voids before priming. When painting this house I wanted to keep the illusion of the false entrance to the doghouse, so after painting the front black I colored the inner surface of the entrance hole using a black marker, which makes the hole almost invisible. We'll use this same technique in the Camera Birdhouse project later in this section. Unlike paint, the marker won't chip off and create a possible hazard for the house residents.

I added two doggie touches to complete the house. The dog bowl is easily created by cutting the rounded bottom off a hardwood candle holder from the craft store (sometimes sold as a candle "cup"), and gluing it to one corner of the base. To prevent the bowl from collecting rainwater, once the glue has dried insert a drill into the bowl and drill a hole right through the base so rain passes through. The last touch was to add the dog name to a small plywood plaque glued to the house front.

FIGURE 1 Start by drawing the doghouse pattern onto the ¼" stock that comprises the false front of the house.

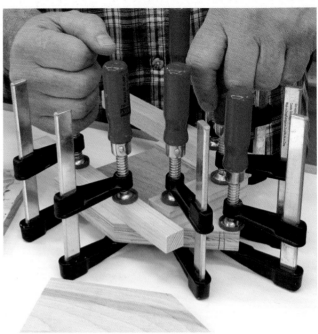

FIGURE 2 Glue the false front to the main house front. Note that I've used wood blocks as clamping cauls to evenly distribute the pressure.

FIGURE 3 Using waterproof glue and nails, attach the house sides to the back first, then attach the house front to the assembly.

FIGURE 4 Attach the right roof half with glue and nails so that the top edge is even with the roof crown. Then attach the left roof half, which overlaps the top edge of the right half.

DOG HOUSE • inches (millimeters)

REFERENCE	QUANTITY	PART	STOCK	THICKNESS	(mm)	WIDTH	(mm)	LENGTH	(mm)	COMMENTS
A	2	front/back	plywood	$1/2$	13	6	152	7	178	
B	2	sides	plywood	$1/2$	13	5	127	$4^1/2$	114	
C	1	left roof	plywood	$1/2$	13	$5^1/2$	140	$7^1/4$	184	
D	1	right roof	plywood	$1/2$	13	5	127	$7^1/4$	184	
E	1	base	plywood	$1/2$	13	8	203	9	229	
F	1	false front	plywood	$1/4$	6	6	152	7	178	
G	1	name plaque	plywood	$1/8$	3	$5/8$	16	$1^1/2$	38	
H	1	dog bowl (a)	hardwood							

a - Dog bowl is made from small hardwood candle holder, cut in half.

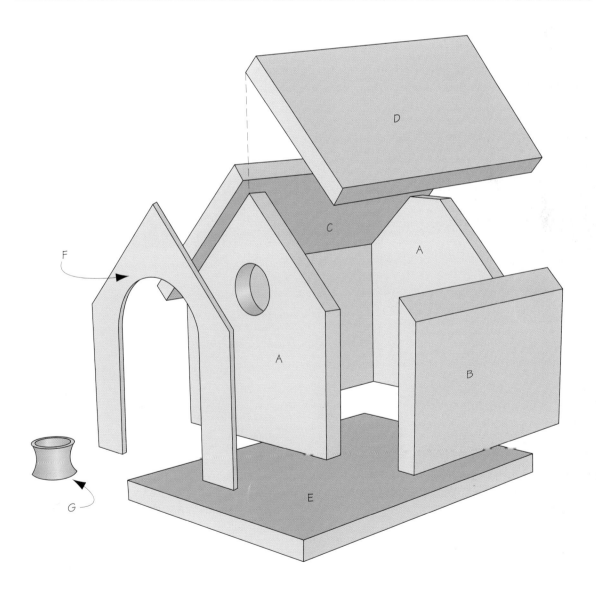

camera house

BACK IN THE DAYS BEFORE DIGITAL TECHNOLOGY put tiny cameras into our shirt pockets, the most popular camera was the bulky, boxy Kodak Brownie. No adjustments, no focusing, no flash and no batteries, the camera was simplicity itself. A hinged rear door gave access to the inside, and putting in film was an often-arduous task of threading loose film onto a spindle, followed by lots and lots of knob twisting to advance the film. A small red window on the back showed how many shots you had left (little numbers were printed on the film), and composing the shot was done by looking through a pair of hazy rectangular lenses. You looked in the top one when shooting vertically, and through the one on the side when tilting the camera for a horizontal shot.

Although the real cameras were almost big enough to make into birdhouses, I've altered the dimensions and proportions a bit for this easy project. Made of ½" pine and assorted hardwood and plywood trim, this house is basically a simple box, much like the original camera was — it's the trim that transforms the appearance into that of a classic antique.

Cut all the house components to size, and cut the two corners off the front of the floor for drainage. Using the front placement pattern as a guide, mark the camera front for the locations of the trim and entrance hole. Use a 2" hardwood disc for the camera lens ring, gluing and clamping it to the camera front where indicated. For the two viewfinder lenses, I used 1¼"- diameter hardwood checkers, available at any craft supply store. These checkers have a raised portion on the underside that allows them to be stacked when playing, but I sanded these off so the backs were perfectly flat before gluing them to the camera front. When everything is dry, drill the entrance hole in a two-step procedure. First, use a Forstner bit to drill a shallow 1½" hole to create the lens ring. Then drill a 1⅛" entrance hole all the way through the front. You can see the finished front in Fig. 1.

Now it's just a matter of assembling the box. With waterproof glue and nails, attach the two sides to the top, then insert the house bottom between the sides and glue and nail it into place, making sure that the two notched corners are to the front. Lay the house on its back, and attach the front, as in Fig. 2.

Flip the house over and attach the hinged door. You'll note in Fig. 3 that the door is sized to created a narrow gap at the top for ventilation. The trim attached to the front may cause the house to wobble a bit when placed face-down like this, but you can see in Fig. 3 that I've balanced it by slipping a couple extra discs at the corners to keep it steady. With the door attached, glue a small piece of ½"-thick scrap to the inside of the top to act as a stop that will keep the door flush as shown in Fig. 4. When the glue has dried, drill a countersunk pilot hole through the top of the door and into this stop, then secure the door closed with a 1" screw.

Using the illustrations and this project's lead photo as a guide, create and place the trim on the camera. The two viewfinders consist of a ³⁄₁₆" × ¾" × 1¼" "lens" made of pine, glued to a thin piece of plywood. Before gluing the lenses in place, I sanded the tops in a soft arch like the originals. The film winder on the side is another of those hardwood checkers. I used a hacksaw blade to cut notches around the edge to simulate the metal winding knob. The shutter button is just a small rectangle of ⅛" plywood. And although it's not seen in any of these photos, I even glued a ¾" hardwood disc on the back, which I painted red to represent the film window. The carrying handle (attached after everything was painted) is a strip of leather cut from an unused belt, drilled on each end to accept hardwood axles from the craft supply store. Painted silver and glued into a pair of holes on top of the camera, they look convincingly like the original metal bolts used on the old cameras. (Fig. 5.)

I painted the camera black (the originals were covered in black leather), all the components that would have been metal a silver color, and the "glass" of the various lenses a glossy gray. To make the entrance hole less obvious, I used a black marker to darken the wood.

FIGURE 1 Drill a 1⅛" entrance hole all the way through the front.

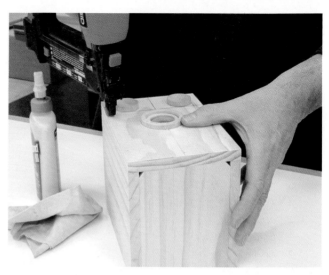

FIGURE 2 Lay the house on its back, and attach the front.

FIGURE 3 Flip the house over and attach the hinged door. Note that the door is sized to created a narrow gap at the top for ventilation.

FIGURE 4 Glue a small piece of ½"-thick scrap to the inside of the top to act as a stop that will keep the door flush with the edges.

FIGURE 5 Painted silver and glued into a pair of holes on top of the camera, the axles look convincingly like the original metal bolts used on the old cameras.

CAMERA HOUSE • inches (millimeters)

REFERENCE	QUANTITY	PART	STOCK	THICKNESS	(mm)	WIDTH	(mm)	LENGTH	(mm)	COMMENTS
A	1	floor	pine	$1/2$	13	4	102	$5^1/_2$	140	
B	2	sides	pine	$1/2$	13	$5^1/_2$	140	7	178	
C	1	front	pine	$1/2$	13	5	127	$7^1/_2$	191	
D	1	top	pine	$1/2$	13	6	152	$5^1/_2$	140	
E	1	back/door	pine	$1/2$	13	4	102	$6^3/_8$	162	
F	1	film winder knob (a)	wood disc			$1^1/_4$ d	32			
G	2	viewfinder assembly (b)	plywood/pine							
H	1	handle	leather	$7/8$	22			$5^1/_4$	133	
I	1	camera lens ring	wood disc	$1/8$	3	2 d	51			
J	2	viewfinder lens (a)	wood disc							
K	2	handle bolts (c)	hardwood							
L	1	shutter button	plywood	$1/8$	3	$3/8$	10	$5/8$	16	
M	1	rear film "window"	wood disc	$1/8$	3	$3/4$	19			

a - $1^1/_4$ diameter hardwood "checker" piece from a craft-supply store.

b - Assembly is $3/_{16} \times 3/_4 \times 1^1/_4$ pine "lens" glued to $1/_{16} \times 1 \times 1^1/_2$ plywood.

c - Standard hardwood "axle" peg from a craft-supply store.

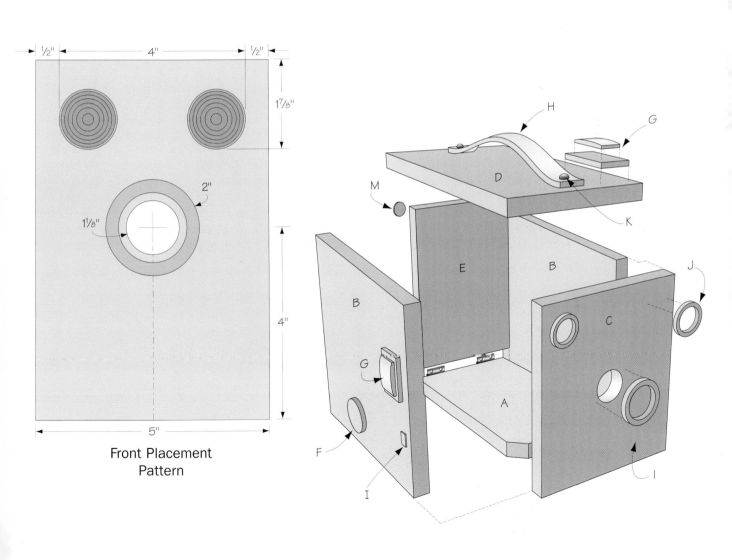

Front Placement
Pattern

cottage

EVERYONE LOVES A COZY COTTAGE, EVEN OUR feathered friends. Based on the basic construction of the Finch House project presented earlier in the book, this cottage is ideal for any bird from tiny wrens up to house finches — just adjust the size of the entrance hole. Smaller birds will find the house roomier than they're used to, but they'll adjust quickly.

Since this cottage is modeled after the Finch House, you'll find that many of the components are similar to those for that project, with some even being the same size. However, where the Finch House was made entirely with ¾" cedar, this one uses a mix of materials from ½" plywood to ⅛"-thick plywood trim for windows and doors. I've taken decorating this house to the extreme by adding thin clapboard siding and cedar shingles, but feel free to do without those touches for a simpler, faster project by just skipping over those steps.

Lay out cutlines for the components on your stock as in Fig. 1. After marking, I cut this workpiece in half right through the center of the "X", then attached the two pieces together to cut the roof angles on both pieces at the same time. (I've done that throughout this book for identical pieces.) As with the Finch House, this one also has a 90° crown, so the house sides are beveled at 45° on their top edges, while the front and back components are cut to a tapered point at 45° angles on each side. When you have the front and back completed, cut ½" off the pointed top of the back workpiece for a ventilation opening.

Unlike the Finch House, the cottage does not have a pivoting side for access (access here will be through the removable base). So, start assembly by attaching the front and back of the house to the two sides with waterproof glue and nails, as shown in Fig. 2.

If you're adding siding, measure and mark it to fit as in Fig. 3. With a piece of scrap underneath, use a sharp utility knife (or a fine-cut saw) to cut your siding to size.

Before attaching the siding, glue and clamp a hardwood disc of the appropriate size for your intended

occupants about 6" up the front of the house; the process here is the same as for the Lighthouse in an earlier chapter. This cottage is for wrens — one of my favorites — so I used a 1¾" disc and drilled a 1⅛" hole through its center. But again, the 5½" × 6½" floor of this house can accommodate a wide range of birds so use a disc of whatever size you prefer and drill the appropriate hole.

Start the siding on the back of the house. Spread a thin layer of glue over the area where the first piece of siding will go as in Fig. 5. Press the siding into place. Place a piece of scrap large enough to cover the siding and clamp in place around the edges until dry. Attaching siding can be a slow process, as you need to wait for the glue to set before moving on to the next piece. I've found that because the glue is spread in such thin layers, you can usually unclamp and move to the next piece after about 20-25 minutes. When the first piece is dry, spread more glue on the next section and press the next piece of siding in place, butting it up against the first. Clamp as before. Move on up the back of the house, and trim off the overhang at the edges of the roof line.

Although you could add windows and doors right on top of the clapboard siding, because the siding is channeled there's always an opportunity for water to get underneath. For that reason I've opted to add my doors and windows first, and fit the siding around them. This involves a lot of cutting and fitting, but the effort is worth it, and the process of priming and painting will do a great job of sealing all edges. I've created my own windows here using ⅛" plywood, as you can see in Fig. 6. However, you can find a huge variety of ready-made (and quite fancy) doors and windows through any dollhouse supplier.

Glue your door and windows in place, and then it's just a matter of cutting and fitting smaller pieces of siding around them as in Fig. 7. Work your way up the sides and front of the house. In Fig. 8, you can see how I've cut the siding to fit around the entrance ring. I used a spare hardwood disc to first trace the circular outline on the siding, and then cut it out with a sharp utility knife. Note in this photo that I didn't put siding between the windows and doors; instead, I'll put shutters there — it's a lot easier than cutting thin strips of siding and getting the clapboard aligned correctly.

Starting with the narrower roof side, apply glue to the angled edges of the side, front and back, then align the roof carefully and nail it into place. (As with the Finch House, start on either side.) Do the same on the other side and nail that half of the roof in place.

Although it's a bit time-consuming, applying cedar shingles — available from any dollhouse supplier — is very easy. First, seal the roof of the house thoroughly with a good primer. Then, mark parallel lines down each side of the roof at a distance determined by the length of the shingles. The shingles you get may recommend a specific overlap of each row, but overlapping ³⁄₈" is about right for most. You can use regular wood-working glue to attach shingles, but if you ever need to repair the roof, removing damaged shingles is a real pain. For that reason, I opted for hot-melt glue, which not only makes the job of hanging shingles much faster, it's far easier to remove a damaged shingle and replace it. (Fig. 9) The last step for the roof after attaching shingles is to add a pair of ¹⁄₈"-thick cedar trim strips on either side of the roof crown.

Now it's just a matter of priming and painting the house any way you prefer, then adding the shutters and whatever trim you'd like, such as the doorknob you see in the final photo. You can find all manner of trim at a dollhouse supplier: brass doorknobs and mail slots, porch lights, weathervanes, you name it.

Finally, mount the cottage to the base by driving four screws up through the bottom and into the assembly. A few ¹⁄₄" or ³⁄₈" holes drilled through the base provide drainage.

There are endless variations you can make to this birdhouse — size, structure, colors, trim and more. Because I've designed this house with a roof that overhangs on all four sides, it's best mounted on a pole using one of the methods described in Part One of this book. If you'd prefer to mount it flush on a tree trunk, alter the construction so that the roof and base do not overhang in the back.

As I mentioned earlier, you don't have to go through all the effort to add the siding and roofing shingles, which admittedly takes a long time. This cottage house would look just as nice with a simple, attractive paint job. But if you do go the extra mile, you've not only created an attractive birdhouse. You may have created an heirloom.

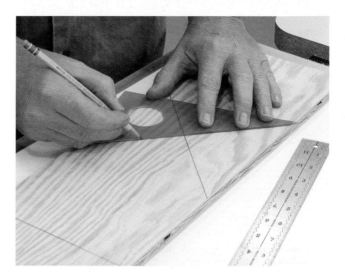

FIGURE 1 Lay out the cutlines for the front/back parts.

FIGURE 2 Start assembly by attaching the front and back of the house to the two sides with waterproof glue and nails.

FIGURE 3 If you're adding siding, now is the time to do it.

COTTAGE • inches (millimeters)

REFERENCE	QUANTITY	PART	STOCK	THICKNESS	(mm)	WIDTH	(mm)	LENGTH	(mm)	COMMENTS
A	2	front/back	plywood	1/2	13	6 1/2	165	8 1/4	209	
B	2	sides	plywood	1/2	13	5 1/2	140	6 1/2	165	
C	1	left roof	plywood	1/2	13	5 1/4	133	9 3/4	248	
D	1	right roof	plywood	1/2	13	5 3/4	146	9 3/4	248	
E	1	bottom	pine	3/4	19	7 1/4	184	8 3/4	402	
F	1	entrance ring	hardwood disc	3/16	5	1 3/4 d	45			

All windows and doors constructed of 1/8" plywood. Roof crown trim strips are 1/8" cedar.
Basswood clapboard siding and cedar shingles are available through dollhouse suppliers.

FIGURE 4 With a piece of scrap underneath, use a sharp utility knife (or a fine-cut saw) to cut your siding to size.

FIGURE 5 Spread a thin layer of glue over the area where the first piece of siding will go.

FIGURE 6 I used ⅛" plywood to make my windows and door.

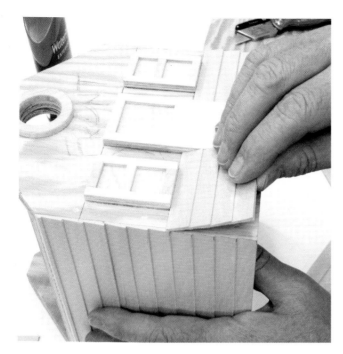

FIGURE 7 Glue your door and windows in place, and then it's just a matter of cutting and fitting smaller pieces of siding around them.

FIGURE 8 I didn't put siding between the windows and doors; instead, I'll put shutters there.

FIGURE 9 I opted for hot-melt glue, which not only makes the job of hanging shingles much faster, it's far easier to remove a damaged shingle and replace it.

SUPPLIERS

ADAMS & KENNEDY —
THE WOOD SOURCE
6178 Mitch Owen Rd.
P.O. Box 700
Manotick, ON
Canada K4M 1A6
613-822-6800
www.wood-source.com
Wood supply

B&Q
Portswood House
1 Hampshire Corporate Park
Chandlers Ford
Eastleigh
Hampshire, England SO53 3YX
0845 609 6688
www.diy.com
Woodworking tools, supplies
and hardware

BUSY BEE TOOLS
130 Great Gulf Dr.
Concord, ON
Canada L4K 5W1
1-800-461-2879
www.busybeetools.com
Woodworking tools and supplies

CONSTANTINE'S WOOD CENTER
OF FLORIDA
1040 E. Oakland Park Blvd.
Fort Lauderdale, FL 33334
800-443-9667
www.constantines.com
Tools, woods, veneers, hardware

FRANK PAXTON LUMBER
COMPANY
5701 W. 66th St.
Chicago, IL 60638
800-323-2203
www.paxtonwood.com
Wood, hardware, tools, books

HOBBY LOBBY
www.hobbylobby.com
craft and art supplies for
any hobby

THE HOME DEPOT
2455 Paces Ferry Rd. NW
Atlanta, GA 30339
800-430-3376 (U.S.)
800-628-0525 (Canada)
www.homedepot.com
Woodworking tools, supplies
and hardware

KLINGSPOR ABRASIVES INC.
2555 Tate Blvd. SE
Hickory, N.C. 28602
800-645-5555
www.klingspor.com
Sandpaper of all kinds

LEE VALLEY TOOLS LTD.
P.O. Box 1780
Ogdensburg, NY 13669-6780
800-871-8158 (U.S.)
800-267-8767 (Canada)
www.leevalley.com
Woodworking tools and hardware

LOWE'S COMPANIES, INC.
P.O. Box 1111
North Wilkesboro, NC 28656
800-445-6937
www.lowes.com
Woodworking tools, supplies
and hardware

MICHAEL'S
www.michaels.com
craft and art supplies for
any hobby

ROCKLER WOODWORKING
AND HARDWARE
4365 Willow Dr.
Medina, MN 55340
800-279-4441
www.rockler.com
Woodworking tools, hardware
and books

TOOL TREND LTD.
140 Snow Blvd. Unit 1
Concord, ON
Canada L4K 4C1
416-663-8665
Woodworking tools and hardware

TREND MACHINERY & CUTTING
TOOLS LTD.
Odhams Trading Estate
St. Albans Rd.
Watford
Hertfordshire, U.K.
WD24 7TR
01923 224657
www.trendmachinery.co.uk
Woodworking tools and hardware

WATERLOX COATINGS
908 Meech Ave.
Cleveland, OH 44105
800-321-0377
www.waterlox.com
Finishing supplies

WOODCRAFT SUPPLY LLC
1177 Rosemar Rd.
P.O. Box 1686
Parkersburg, WV 26102
800-535-4482
www.woodcraft.com
Woodworking hardware

WOODWORKER'S HARDWARE
P.O. Box 180
Sauk Rapids, MN 56379-0180
800-383-0130
www.wwhardware.com
Woodworking hardware

WOODWORKER'S SUPPLY
1108 N. Glenn Rd.
Casper, WY 82601
800-645-9292
http://woodworker.com
Woodworking tools and acces-
sories, finishing supplies, books
and plans

INDEX

More great titles from Popular Woodworking

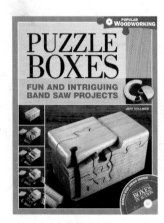

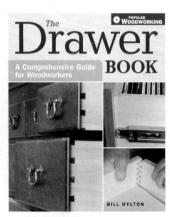

PUZZLE BOXES
by Jeff Vollmer

Have you ever thought *inside* the box? The author has described his boxes and key-and-slide — cut a dovetail, cut a slider piece, cut another key, cut another slider. That's the puzzle or "combination" you use to get to the chamber or heart of the box. *Puzzle Boxes* includes a DVD where Jeff shows you how to set up your band saw and cutout, glue up, sand and fit and finish these amazing boxes.

ISBN 13: 978-1-55870-847-1
ISBN 10: 1-55870-847-2,
hardcover w/DVD, 144 p.,
#Z2116

THE DRAWER BOOK
by Bill Hylton

The Drawer Book is encyclopedic in its content. Author Bill Hylton shows you the professional skills used to:
· construct all styles of drawers
· make and use every kind of drawer-making joint
· create wooden drawer slides and guides
· fit and finish drawers
A live-action DVD gives you all the information you need to choose commercially-manufactured drawer slides. You'll learn how to install the right hardware for the job.

ISBN 13: 978-1-55870-842-6
ISBN 10: 1-55870-842-1,
hardcover w/spiral, 160 p., #Z2007

THE PERFECT EDGE
by Ron Hock

If you've never experienced the pleasure of using a really sharp tool, you're missing one of the real pleasures of woodworking. The mystery of the elusive sharp edge is solved. This book covers all the different sharpening methods so you can improve your sharpening techniques using your existing set-up or determine which one will best suet your needs and budget.

ISBN 13: 978-1-55870-858-7
ISBN 10: 1-55870-858-8,
hardcover, 224 p., #Z2676

BOX MAKING BONANZA
DVD-ROM

Boxes are the perfect projects for any woodworker. They offer an excellent opportunity to learn, practice and master many of the techniques and joinery used in all woodworking and furniture-making projects. These projects are great for using scrap lumber left over from other projects, or exotic woods that would be too costly the use in a larger project.

ISBN 13: 978-1-55870-864-5
This disc includes the full book content from: *Box by Box, Creating Beautiful Boxes with Inlay Techniques, Simply Beautiful Boxes*, DVD-ROM, #Z4824

THESE AND OTHER GREAT WOODWORKING BOOKS ARE AVAILABLE AT YOUR LOCAL BOOKSTORE, WOODWORKING STORES OR FROM ONLINE SUPPLIERS.

www.popularwoodworking.com